Familiarity and Conviction in the Criminal Justice System

American Psychology-Law Society Series

Books in the Series

Expert Testimony on the Psychology of Eyewitness Identification
Edited by Brian L. Cutler

The Psychology of Judicial Decision-Making
Edited by David Klein and Gregory Mitchell

The Miranda Ruling: Its Past, Present, and Future
Lawrence S. Wrightsman and Mary L. Pitman

Juveniles at Risk: A Plea for Preventive Justice
Christopher Slobogin and Mark R. Fondacaro

The Ethics of Total Confinement
Bruce A. Arrigo, Heather Y. Bersot, and Brian G. Sellers

International Human Rights and Mental Disability Law
Michael L. Perlin

Applying Social Science to Reduce Violent Offending
Edited by Joel Dvoskin, Jennifer L. Skeem, Raymond W. Novaco, and Kevin S. Douglas

Children Who Resist Postseparation Parental Contact
Barbara Jo Fidler, Nicholas Bala, and Michael A. Saini

Trauma, Stress, and Wellbeing in the Legal System
Edited by Monica K. Miller and Brian H. Bornstein

Psychology, Law, and the Wellbeing of Children
Edited by Monica K. Miller, Jared C. Chamberlain, and Twila Wingrove

Murder in the Courtroom: The Cognitive Neuroscience of Extreme Violent Behavior
Brigitte Vallabhajosula

Rational Suicide, Irrational Laws: Examining Current Approaches to Suicide in Policy and Law
Susan Stefan

International Perspectives on Violence Risk Assessment
Edited by Jay P. Singh, Stål Bjørkly, and Seena Fazel

Adolescence, Privacy, and the Law: A Developmental Science Perspective
Roger J.R. Levesque

The Ethical Practice of Forensic Psychology
Gianni Pirelli, Robert A. Beattey, and Patricia A. Zapf

The Jury Under Fire: Myth, Controversy, and Reform
Brian H. Bornstein and Edie Greene

The Science and Law of School Segregation and Diversity
Roger J.R. Levesque

Criminal Juries in the 21st Century: Contemporary Issues, Psychological Science, and the Law
Edited by Cynthia J. Najdowski and Margaret C. Stevenson

The Behavioral Science of Firearms
Gianni Pirelli, Hayley Wechsler, and Robert J. Cramer

A System of Pleas
Edited by Vanessa A. Edkins and Allison D. Redlich

Hugo Münsterberg's Psychology and Law: A Historical and Contemporary Assessment
Brian H. Bornstein and Jeffrey S. Neuschatz

Familiarity and Conviction in the Criminal Justice System

Definitions, Theory, and Eyewitness Research

Joanna Pozzulo, Emily Pica,

and Chelsea Sheahan

OXFORD
UNIVERSITY PRESS

OXFORD
UNIVERSITY PRESS

Oxford University Press is a department of the University of Oxford. It furthers the University's objective of excellence in research, scholarship, and education by publishing worldwide. Oxford is a registered trade mark of Oxford University Press in the UK and certain other countries.

Published in the United States of America by Oxford University Press
198 Madison Avenue, New York, NY 10016, United States of America.

Library of Congress Control Number: 2019949806
ISBN 978-0-19-087481-0

9 8 7 6 5 4 3 2 1

Printed by Marquis, Canada

Contents

Series Foreword

This book series is sponsored by the American Psychology-Law Society (AP-LS; https://www.apadivisions.org/division-41/index). AP-LS is an interdisciplinary organization devoted to scholarship, practice, and public service in psychology and law. Its goals include advancing the contributions of psychology to the understanding of law and legal institutions through basic and applied research; promoting the education of psychologists in matters of law and the education of legal personnel in matters of psychology; and informing the psychological and legal communities and the general public of current research, educational, and service activities in the field of psychology and law. AP-LS membership includes psychologists from the academic, research, and clinical practice communities as well as members of the legal community. Research and practice are represented in both the civil and criminal legal arenas. AP-LS has chosen Oxford University Press as a strategic partner because of its commitment to scholarship, quality, and the international dissemination of ideas. These strengths will help AP-LS reach its goal of educating the psychology and legal professions and the general public about important developments in psychology and law. The focus of the book series reflects the diversity of the field of psychology and law, as we will publish books on a broad range of topics.

In the latest book in the series, *Familiarity and Conviction in the Criminal Justice System: Definitions, Theory, and Eyewitness Research*, Joanna Pozzulo, Emily Pica, and Chelsea Sheahan have synthesized the available research and literature on familiarity and its application within the context of eyewitness evidence. The authors infuse this synthesis with real-life cases involving familiar strangers as a means of delineating the role of familiarity in eyewitness identification and discussing the ways in which it might influence eyewitness evidence. The result is an accessible volume that provides a sound rationale for the importance of considering familiarity in eyewitness evidence and in eyewitness research.

Pozzulo, Pica, and Sheahan begin with a compilation of real-life cases involving familiar strangers and a discussion of the construct of familiarity. They describe the theoretical underpinnings, from social psychological and cognitive perspectives, and factors that can interact with familiarity, including both system variables and estimator variables. Consideration is then given to familiarity as a dependent variable and to the persuasiveness of an eyewitnesses who is familiar with the defendant. The authors conclude by providing directions for future research on the notion of familiarity and its impact on the criminal justice system.

Familiarity and Conviction in the Criminal Justice System: Definitions, Theory, and Eyewitness Research presents a detailed analysis of the influence of familiarity on eyewitness evidence and will undoubtedly be a compelling read for researchers, legal professionals, and testifying experts alike.

Patricia A. Zapf
Series Editor

Preface

All three of us are fascinated with news stories that involve an "eyewitness." The resolution of the crimes we hear about on the news often ends with a perpetrator who was *known* to the eyewitness or victim. A few years ago, it occurred to us that the majority of eyewitness research, both generally and specifically, focused on a *stranger as a perpetrator*. There was a disconnect between the research and real life. We started to ask ourselves, "Does knowing the perpetrator make a difference in terms of description or identification accuracy compared to when the perpetrator is a stranger?" Sure, if the perpetrator was someone very well known to the eyewitness–victim, then in all likelihood knowing the person would help with description and identification. Moreover, it is fair to ask whether description and identification evidence is even relevant when one *knows* the perpetrator. But there is a middle ground when the perpetrator *may* have been seen before, in a different context, or may be someone the eyewitness–victim interacted with on one or two occasions. How would these scenarios impact describing and identifying the perpetrator? Given that the majority of research and conclusions made concerning eyewitness identification accuracy are based on the notion of a stranger-perpetrator, it is important to examine whether differences arise between a stranger and familiar identification to determine whether best practice recommendations need to be modified.

Our starting point was a desire to conduct eyewitness research that more closely mirrored relationships between an eyewitness–victim and perpetrator that are seen in real-life crime and understand how that relationship influences an eyewitness' accuracy. Our curiosity also batted around how the general public perceived the accuracy of an eyewitness–victim when a claim of knowing the perpetrator was made. We set out on a program of eyewitness research that manipulated the degree of familiarity between the eyewitness and the perpetrator. We quickly realized that we could operationalize familiarity a multitude of ways—number of previous exposures, types of exposure, quality of exposure, type of relationship, and so on. We almost as quickly realized that what we thought made for a "more familiar" perpetrator was not necessarily what our participant–eyewitnesses thought. Perhaps people's perceptions would drive their decision-making both as eyewitnesses and as jurors in juror decision-making studies.

A few things happened somewhat simultaneously. First, a number of studies we conducted suggested familiarity in an eyewitness context was an elusive concept to measure and the results were not always consistent with what we thought would happen. Second, other researchers were contacting us about our familiarity studies because they too were interested in the topic and wanted to know how we were conducting our studies. Last, we were being contacted by lawyers searching for information on the topic of familiar eyewitnesses. These three factors were the impetus for us to decide that the time was right to pull together all the research we could find that examined familiarity in an eyewitness context.

Our goal with this book was to summarize the psychological literature as it relates to an eyewitness—victim who claims to have some familiarity with the perpetrator. We wanted to define what is meant by "familiarity" in an eyewitness context, how it has been operationalized and manipulated, explore factors that may interact with familiarity, and examine jurors' perceptions of familiarity. Eyewitness research often crosses social psychology as well as cognitive psychology, and as such, we dedicated a chapter per area to illuminate the various approaches to understanding familiarity. We also considered it important to discuss how an eyewitness may believe they are familiar with the perpetrator but are mistaken. Last, we wanted to provide some suggestions on where we think the field should go at this point.

It was important to us to give the reader a sense of how familiarity has impacted real-life cases. A number of real-life cases in which familiarity was claimed by the eyewitness are described in Chapter 1. In addition, in the following chapters, we highlight real-life cases that illustrate the factors that researchers have undertaken to examine. It is critical to keep in mind that claims of familiarity in real-life may or may not be accurate. Moreover, descriptions and identifications following claims of familiarity may or may not be accurate. Therefore, it is imperative to understand how familiarity influences eyewitness accuracy.

We hope the reader will come away with a greater appreciation for the challenges of conducting research in the area of eyewitness–perpetrator familiarity. It may be a far reach to generalize this research to real-life cases, but it may be a closer approximation compared to the research using a stranger identification paradigm. We encourage researchers to include familiarity as a manipulation as we try to conduct ethically sound and relevant research with the ultimate goal of providing best practices for the collection of eyewitness evidence when there may be some familiarity between the eyewitness and the perpetrator.

Familiarity and Conviction in the Criminal Justice System

1

Defining Familiarity and Overview of Concepts

For more than 100 years, eyewitness research has focused almost exclusively on stranger identification. It makes sense to consider that "identification of the perpetrator" is most informative in the stranger situation. If you see your uncle Jim commit a crime, identification is less of an issue: the perpetrator is uncle Jim. Thus, identification seems most informative in a stranger situation. That is, someone unbeknownst to the eyewitness/victim commits a crime and needs to be identified. However, identification is also critical for the *familiar-stranger*. Consider a perpetrator who you think you have seen previously walk his dog in the park. Many identifications fall somewhere between the two extremes of *familiar* and *stranger*. This book explores this "middle ground" as it relates to the criminal justice system. Understanding the influence of familiarity on descriptions and identifications and the factors that can interact with familiarity is critical in order to evaluate this sort of eyewitness evidence. This chapter describes the familiarity construct, how it has been manipulated and measured, and provides descriptions of real-life cases in which the defendant was considered familiar to the eyewitness/victim.

Familiarity Construct

> "I've seen him around the neighborhood. I often see him at the coffee shop reading the local newspaper and having a coffee. I've never spoken to him."
>
> "She works at the bank. I've gone to her a few times to cash my checks."
>
> "I've nodded to him on my morning jog."

Familiarity and Conviction in the Criminal Justice System. Joanna Pozzulo, Emily Pica, and Chelsea Sheahan, Oxford University Press (2020).
DOI: 10.1093/oso/9780190874810.001.0001

"I've seen her before. I think she is a cashier at the grocery store."

"The gossip magazines always report on the Royal Family. I feel like I know the Royals."

Familiarity is an elusive concept. It can be a sense of knowing someone or a sense of having had exposure to someone in a prior context, perhaps in a different context. You may have seen someone previously or spoken to him or her but not know his or her name. Then, when you see that person in another context, you believe it is that same person you had seen or known previously. You may have interacted with someone, once or many times before, so you feel you know the person, *a little*. You may have had an opportunity to learn about a person, such as a celebrity, but you have never met the person. This sense of knowing also can lead to a sense of familiarity.

Familiarity can occur on a continuum, on one end of which you have high familiarity with the person—that is, you have seen the person in many contexts and have had several different interactions with the person. Examples on this end of the continuum are a parent, loved one, or best friend. On the other end of the continuum is someone you have never seen before—someone who is completely unknown. You have not had any prior type of contact with the person nor have you had any exposure to the person. This person is a "stranger." In between these two extremes are individuals with whom you have some "degree of familiarity," or "a sense of familiarity." Examples include the mail carrier who you see drop off your mail on occasion and remark on the weather, a barista who often makes your coffee at the local coffee shop, a teacher from your elementary school years, a co-worker at the same company at which you work but with whom you do not interact regularly, someone who works in your building with whom you ride the elevator in the morning, and the movie star on whom you have a crush. Numerous other examples are possible. Think of the number of people to whom you have "exposure" on a daily, weekly, yearly basis. We use the term *familiar-stranger* to denote these types of individuals who fall in the middle of the continuum scale of "familiarity" between those we know extremely well and those who are complete strangers.

Defining the Construct of Familiarity

As the previous examples illustrate, there are various aspects to the concept of familiarity. Familiarity includes a sense of "knowing" and/or "seeing" someone previously. You have had exposure to someone in one context, and you believe it is this same person in another context or on another occasion. According to the *APA Dictionary of Psychology* (https://dictionary.apa.org/familiarity), familiarity invokes "a subjective feeling of recognition." In a criminal context, you witness someone commit a crime, and you believe it is someone with whom you are "familiar." It is your high school gym teacher or the older gentleman who you have seen in the park on the weekend.

According to a layman dictionary (https://www.yourdictionary.com), familiarity is defined as knowledge of someone or something, or a feeling of comfort and closeness with someone or something. People's use of the term "familiar" provides opportunity to demonstrate individual differences where one person may require a higher threshold for the label "familiar" compared with someone else. A co-worker may say, "I don't really *know* Bob. He occupies the cubicle across from me and we just greet each other in the morning." Alternatively, someone may say, "I *know* Bob. He lives across the street from me. We always say hello." To some degree, a sense of "knowing" seems to be part of the familiarity construct. In addition, having some prior exposure to the individual in some way (e.g., live or via media) is essential. The degree, type, quantity, and quality of these familiarity elements are currently being empirically investigated, but a consensus on a definition of "familiarity," particularly in a criminal justice application, has not yet been reached.

How Do We Measure and Manipulate Familiarity?

In a typical eyewitness study, an unsuspecting participant is shown an unfamiliar target, live or on video, and is later asked to describe that target. Following that, a "lineup" (i.e., a set of photos) is shown to the participant for identification of that target. If one is interested in studying the accuracy of identifying a target who is a familiar-stranger, a manipulation of familiarity would need to occur prior to asking a witness to describe and identify the target.

A number of familiarity manipulations have been used throughout the literature with varying influences on identification. Here, we detail the examples we found and their impact on identification.

Subjective Feeling

Examining the construct of familiarity, Steblay, Dietrich, Ryan, Raczynski, and James (2011) had participants view a video of a confederate stealing a purse. The confederate was a graduate of the school at which the participants were students, thus allowing for familiarity with the confederate to be measured. That is, participants were asked if they had seen the confederate before and were then grouped into those who said they were familiar and those who said they were not familiar with the confederate. After the video, participants were shown a lineup and had the option of reviewing the lineup twice. Participants who stated they were familiar with the confederate were more likely to correctly identify him than were participants who stated they had not seen the confederate previously. When shown a target-absent lineup (i.e., the confederate was not among the photos shown), those familiar with the confederate were more accurate than those who were unfamiliar with the confederate. In this study, using a subjective measure of familiarity was associated with greater identification accuracy, both for identifying and for correctly rejecting a lineup.

Prior Exposure

Familiarity also has been manipulated in terms of number of "prior exposures." For example, facial images are flashed on a computer screen, each for a few seconds. Certain faces are flashed more than once. Consider a face interspersed in a series of faces, with the target face shown three times in this sequence of faces. The face shown three times is "more familiar" than a face that is shown only once in the sequence. Hinz and Pezdek (2001) examined how seeing a face multiple times can influence subsequent identification accuracy. Participants were exposed to a target photograph that was accompanied by a story about the individual. In addition, participants were instructed to pay attention to both the story and the photograph because they would have to answer related questions. One week later, participants were provided with one of two intervening lineups: a target-absent lineup or a lineup containing a repeated distractor face (i.e., a foil face that was repeated from the intervening lineup to the actual lineup). Two days later, participants were presented with the actual lineup that was presented in one of three ways: (1) target, repeated distractor face, and five foils; (2) target and five foils; or (3) the repeated distractor face and five foils. Regardless of which lineup participants viewed, they were instructed to identify the man from the story. The participants' accuracy rate was significantly higher when they were shown a target-only lineup compared to the target and repeated distractor face lineup. When participants were shown the lineup with the target face and the repeated distractor face, their accuracy rates were much lower, suggesting that the familiar, repeated face influenced their decision-making. Thus, using this methodology and manipulation, prior exposure to a face, other than the target face, can hinder the ability of an eyewitness to make a correct identification if both faces are present; moreover, it can lead to a higher rate of false alarms if only the familiar, repeated face is present.

Length of Exposure

Related to the number of prior exposures to manipulate familiarity is the length of the exposure. For example, a number of face recognition studies in the cognitive psychology domain have varied exposure time of a target from a few milliseconds to a few seconds or longer (e.g., 30–45 seconds). Some studies with a more applied focus have varied the length of exposure from 1 or 2 minutes to 10–20 minutes. A target who is shown for a longer period of time is presumed more familiar than a target who is shown for a shorter period of time.

Memon, Hope, and Bull (2003) examined whether a longer exposure to a target increases recognition accuracy in target-present (i.e., the target is among the photos) and target-absent lineups (i.e., the target is not among the photos). Using a sample of 164 younger (aged 17–25 years) and older adults (aged 59–81 years) with half the participants being exposed to the target for 12 seconds (short duration) and half being exposed for 45 seconds (long duration), the researchers found that longer exposure to the target increased recognition accuracy compared to the shorter exposure duration. Specifically, participants in the longer exposure duration conditions produced more correct identifications, whereas the participants in the shorter-exposure conditions made more false-positive identifications.

In contrast to the previously discussed laboratory study, using real-life data to examine exposure duration, Horry, Halford, Brewer, Milne, and Bull (2014) reviewed 295 case files from a UK police force. Of these cases, 833 lineups were presented to eyewitnesses. The rate of suspect identification was significantly higher for witnesses who were exposed to the perpetrator for a longer period of time (i.e., more than 60 seconds) than for witnesses who were exposed to the perpetrator for a shorter period of time (i.e., less than 60 seconds). Of course, we are unable to determine if the suspects identified were actually the guilty perpetrators. It appears that a longer exposure duration may increase recognition accuracy. How long of an exposure duration is sufficient for improved recognition accuracy?

In a meta-analysis examining the effects of exposure time on identification accuracy, Bornstein, Deffenbacher, Penrod, and McGorty (2012) reviewed 25 facial recognition studies and found that longer exposure to a perpetrator resulted in significantly greater identification accuracy than did shorter exposure durations (see also Shapiro & Penrod, 1986). Intriguingly, however, Bornstein and colleagues suggested that the effect of exposure time was nonlinear and that the effect of increased exposure may be most influential when exposure time is relatively short. Specifically, the largest effects appear when the exposure time is less than 30 seconds. Once the exposure time exceeds 30 seconds, any further increase would need to be substantially greater to produce an effect. Thus, some prior exposure is helpful for improved recognition accuracy, but at some point additional exposure time does not increase recognition accuracy. For example, meeting a new co-worker and then working alongside that person for 8 hours may not change your ability to recognize her later in the week compared to if you had worked alongside her for 4 hours. However, you can imagine that a number of other factors may interact with exposure duration. Consider that your co-worker gets reassigned to a different department and you do not see her for 6 months: Would you still be able to recognize her? What if she changes her hairstyle? Longer durations beyond 30 seconds may be helpful to improve recognition compared to durations of less than 30 seconds, but the time between exposure and identification may be one factor that changes this conclusion. In all likelihood, a number of factors interact with length of exposure to influence recognition accuracy.

Celebrities

Showing participants images of celebrities compared to strangers is another method that has been employed to examine the impact of "familiarity" on recognition accuracy. A celebrity would be more familiar than a stranger. Greene and Robinson (1993) examined whether participants would be better able to recognize famous (i.e., familiar) individuals compared to men involved in a case (e.g., prior suspects and attorneys) with and without a disguise (i.e., a fedora hat and sunglasses). The primary purpose of the study was to determine whether identification accuracy of familiar faces that were disguised would be inhibited. Participants were shown a series of 11 faces and were asked to write down the name of each person. Each participant saw roughly half of the faces with no disguise and half of the faces with disguise; moreover, each face was shown both with and without a disguise. Results indicated that participants were more likely to identify the famous faces at a higher rate than the unfamiliar faces (Greene & Robinson, 1993). Intriguingly, when famous faces were disguised, identification accuracy decreased. For example, George Bush was recognized at a rate of 100% accuracy without disguise; however, he was only recognized at a rate of 28% accuracy with the disguise. Hence, someone who may be "familiar" but is wearing glasses, for example, becomes an "unfamiliar" face for identification.

In another study employing famous faces for familiar recognition, Clutterbuck and Johnston (2005) examined undergraduate students' reaction time and accuracy when matching pairs of faces that included famous (i.e., known), familiar (i.e., repeated encounters with a novel face), and unfamiliar faces. Clutterbuck and Johnston used a matching task as an indirect measure of familiarity because earlier research has shown that different views of the same face tend to be matched more quickly for familiar faces compared to novel faces (Young, Hay, McWeeny, Flude, & Ellis, 1985). Faces were matched on either interior or exterior features, presented in pairs, and presented either 5 times for 4 seconds each or 10 times for 2 seconds each. Each pair consisted of a famous face, a familiarized face presented 5 times for 4 seconds each, a familiarized face presented 10 times for 2 seconds each, or a never before seen face. Each photograph was paired with the internal or external features removed. Famous or known faces were matched faster on their internal features compared to the familiarized and new faces (Clutterbuck & Johnston, 2005). In addition, in Experiment 2, familiarized faces were matched faster than the new faces. Clutterbuck and Johnston's results shed light on how being familiar with a face can increase accuracy, even when certain facial features are not present. In this context, familiarity again aids recognition accuracy.

High School Yearbook

In some studies, researchers have used photos from participants' old high school yearbooks to compare those who are "familiar" versus strangers to determine the ability of individuals to remember or recall their old high school classmates. Often with these types of studies, researchers are interested in examining memory for faces from more than 20 years ago. In a classic study, Bahrick, Bahrick, and Wittlinger (1975) investigated the influence of familiarity on face recognition. Participants were high school graduates aged 17–74 years who supplied their yearbooks to the research team. Participants were exposed to photocopies of the yearbook photographs from their graduating class. Participants were asked to write down all of the first and last names they could remember as well as participate in a recognition test. The recognition test consisted of presenting the participants with 10 cards that contained five pictures each, one of which was from their graduating class. Participants were asked to identify the picture from their own yearbook. Participants were highly accurate in identifying their former classmates, with the mean accuracy rate of 0.76. Even after many years since graduation (15+ years), participants could accurately identify their former classmates. Of course, it is difficult to assess the quality of contact and extent of exposure between classmates, but it does appear that familiarity remains for numerous years with good recognition accuracy. But is this always the case?

More recently, Pezdek and Stolzenberg (2014) examined students' ability to recognize recent graduates from their high school. Participants were presented with pictures of recent graduates from their school and pictures of students from another nearby school. Results indicated that 23% of the unfamiliar faces were misidentified as being familiar, and only 42% of the familiar faces were correctly identified as being familiar. In addition, familiar faces were significantly more likely to be identified as familiar than were the unfamiliar faces. However, Pezdek and Stolzenberg suggest that the number of faces classified as familiar when they actually had not been seen before suggests that familiarity judgments should be used cautiously in forensic settings. This study does raise concern regarding claims of familiarity; however, familiarity was not experimentally controlled, thus limiting our understanding of the effects of familiarity on identification accuracy in a criminal justice context.

Prior Live Exposure: Brief Interaction

In an attempt to better simulate real-world experience, researchers have performed studies in which a confederate enters a store and asks a sales associate for directions and then leaves the store. Following a delay (e.g., 30 minutes vs. 1 day), a researcher enters the store and asks the sales associate about the individual who asked for directions. In this scenario, the confederate asking for directions is more familiar than a complete stranger. Using this sort of paradigm, Yarmey, Jacob, and Porter (2002) had a confederate approach individuals to ask for assistance in finding jewelry. This interaction lasted either 5 or 30 seconds. Approximately 2 minutes later, participants were given a cued-recall test that included 14 items concerning the confederate's physical characteristics and clothing. Participants in the 30-seconds condition were more accurate in their descriptions of eye color and clothing compared to those in the 5-seconds condition; there were no other significant differences. Again, this shows that a longer interaction of 30 seconds, in this case a live interaction, improves one's recall accuracy.

In a somewhat related scenario, Gross and Hayne (1996) examined the role of a brief, live interaction on children's (5- and 6-year-olds) identification accuracy. Children were exposed to four different confederates. Children interacted with two of these confederates for 1 hour (i.e., long exposure), and children were exposed to the other two for only a few minutes (i.e., short exposure). Gross and Hayne found that when shown a target-present lineup, children were able to correctly identify the two confederates in the long-exposure condition, with whom they interacted, and one of the confederates in the short-exposure condition. With the target-absent lineups, children had difficulty correctly rejecting lineups regardless of exposure duration. These results suggest that children may be more accurate in their identification of familiar-strangers only in target-present lineups. There may be a more general issue occurring whereby children have greater difficulty correctly rejecting lineups regardless of length of exposure (Pozzulo, 2016; Pozzulo & Lindsay, 1998).

Revealing Personal Information

Considering a different aspect of familiarity, some researchers perform studies in which a confederate reveals personal details of oneself in order to induce a sense of familiarity for the confederate. For example, a participant and a confederate engage in an exercise that requires them to share their thoughts or personal experiences on a particular topic (political views, childhood details, etc.). This sharing of information induces a sense of familiarity whereby the person who shared personal information is more familiar than the person who did not share. Researchers then can compare the recall and recognition abilities for a familiar versus unfamiliar confederate versus a stranger using this "sharing" paradigm.

In the first study of its kind, Pettalia (2015) examined whether familiarity influenced identification accuracy using the sharing paradigm. Pettalia operationalized familiarity as a personal interaction and/or knowledge of the target. Participants either interacted with the target for 30 minutes with no personal information revealed or interacted with the target for 30 minutes with personal information of the target revealed. Participants were more likely to produce higher rates of correct identification when the target revealed personal information compared to the stranger condition (i.e., participants had no prior exposure to the target). This study suggests that familiarity may require more than "exposure" to influence identification accuracy as we move closer to real-world scenarios.

Overall, the previous examples illustrate how researchers create and induce a sense of familiarity in their participants. Once this familiarity is established, we can begin to examine the impact it has on recalling individuals and identifying them. It is becoming clear that how we manipulate familiarity may influence the decisions we reach on its impact. When examining the research thus far, it is clear that in many cases, only components of familiarity have been manipulated (e.g., exposure time and personal information). Familiarity, in all likelihood, is composed of a number of components. Herein lies the difficulty of not only experimentally manipulating familiarity but also defining familiarity within the context of the justice system. The lack of a standard definition of what it means to be "familiar" places a limitation on our ability to fully understand how familiarity impacts eyewitness identification. Very generally, the research summarized in this chapter suggests that more familiarity improves eyewitness accuracy, but there may be a point at which more does not further increase accuracy. Moreover, it is also evident that factors may interact with familiarity to influence an eyewitness' accuracy. There also may be conditions in which familiarity hinders an eyewitness' accuracy. Consider the situation in which an eyewitness *thinks* he or she is familiar with the perpetrator but actually is not.

Real-Life Cases Involving a Familiar-Stranger

In this book, the context for familiarity is when an eyewitness has some familiarity of a person in a noncriminal context and then recognizes a perpetrator to be familiar. For example, you see a sketch of someone wanted for a crime against a child in your community and you think you know the wanted person. You believe it is your mail courier. Alternatively, the young man you see grab a woman at the bus shelter is the same young man you have seen riding his bike in the neighborhood. The majority of crime against children and adults is perpetrated by someone with whom the victim has some familiarity (Miethe & Drass, 1999). For example, Flowe, Mehta, and Ebbesen (2011) sampled 725 felony cases in the United States. In the majority of cases (67%), the suspect was familiar (i.e., acquainted) with at least one eyewitness involved in the case. In addition, Gross, Jacoby, Matheson, Montgomery, and Patil (2005) examined all known exonerations that occurred in the United States between 1989 and 2003 ($N = 328$). In 86% of the cases in which defendants were convicted of murder but later exonerated, the defendants were acquainted with one or more of the eyewitnesses who testified at trial.

A high-profile case that provides a salient example of being familiar with the perpetrator is that of Elizabeth Smart's sister, Mary Katherine, who witnessed her sister's abduction and noted, "I heard his voice before" (Smart,

Smart, & Morton, 2003). It took several months for Mary Katherine to place the voice: it was someone who had briefly worked for the Smart family as a gardener. One could argue that the perpetrator was a familiar-stranger. The degree of familiarity between Mary Katherine and the abductor is unclear, however. In addition, it is difficult to ascertain the degree to which Mary Katherine's previous experience with the abductor influenced the accuracy of her identification.

Vallano and Winter (2016) reported that in 2009, a woman was performing her usual duties at an outlet store where she worked. While on duty working, a man entered the store—a man she knew as a "somewhat familiar" customer. He selected some items and then went to the counter to pay for them. During this cash out, he pulled a knife and put it to her throat and demanded she empty the cash register. Once he fled with the money, the woman called the police and gave a description to the investigating officer and said she recognized the perpetrator as one of her "regular customers" (Vallano & Winter, 2016). The description she gave the police matched the suspect, Stanley Williams. Because of her identification, which was shown roughly 2 hours after the incident, Stanley was convicted and sent to prison (*State v. Williams*, 2013). Interestingly, in this case, expert testimony around eyewitness identification issues was excluded because the court decided that a familiar identification holds more merit or value than a stranger identification.

Unfortunately, a sense of familiarity also can be problematic for a suspect. In the case against Clarence Elkins, his 6-year-old niece had witnessed her grandmother being assaulted. When the perpetrator noticed the young child, he followed her to her room and later assaulted her. The next morning, she ran to her neighbor's house to call the police because she had found her grandmother dead; she told the neighbor that the man who attacked her grandmother looked like her uncle, Clarence Elkins (Innocence Project, 2017a). Given that she was the sole eyewitness to the crime, she testified in court that it was her uncle who killed her grandmother. Elkins was convicted on all charges. Approximately 7 years later, he was released because the court acknowledged his innocence after his niece recanted her testimony and DNA evidence excluded him as the perpetrator in the case. Interestingly, the actual perpetrator was found through the help of Elkins and his wife using intuition and teamwork. Elkins' wife had a feeling that a convicted rapist who lived in the same neighborhood as the victim might be the murderer. Ironically, this same man had been jailed and was transferred to the same cell block in which Elkins was housed. One day, Elkins picked up the man's cigarette butt, gave it to his wife, and she had it tested for DNA. The DNA from the cigarette butt matched the DNA from the victim.

Family members are not the only familiar individuals who can wrongfully accuse someone of a crime, however. Walter Snyder served 7 years in prison for a crime he did not commit (Innocence Project, 2017b). In 1985, a woman was attacked during a home invasion. The assailant appeared to have resembled her neighbor, Snyder. When police presented the victim with a showup (i.e., a single photo of a suspect), she identified Snyder as the man who attacked her. The victim remembered seeing Snyder before, as he was her neighbor, and erroneously inferred that her memory of him was as her attacker, not her neighbor who lived across the street. Snyder received an absolute pardon in 1993.

In another case involving a child witness, Johnny Williams spent 14 years in prison for an attempted rape that he did not commit (Innocence Project, 2017c). A 9-year-old girl was accosted while walking home from school. The next day she was attacked; the male referred to himself as "Johnny." Williams was familiar with the girl and her family because he was a former neighbor of theirs. Initially, the young girl stated that she did not know her attacker. However, people in the neighborhood suggested to the police that "Johnny" may be Johnny Williams, who used to live in that area. Interestingly, this case highlights that others who are familiar with someone such as a former neighbor can influence a case. The name Johnny was familiar to those who lived in the neighborhood, so they thought the attacker must have been their former neighbor Johnny. Even a familiar name can lead to a wrongful conviction.

Several other cases point to errors of familiarity. For example, in 1991, two sisters woke up to an intruder in their home who assaulted them. The victims told police that their attacker looked like a man who had previously lived in the area, Joseph Abbitt (National Registry of Exonerations, 2017a). Indeed, Abbitt had been to their home before, as neighbors often do. Abbitt became the primary suspect based on the identification made from both victims. There was no DNA evidence linking Abbitt to the crime; however, he was still convicted, based primarily on the victims' testimonies that the man who attacked them looked like Abbitt, with whom they were familiar. After 14 years in prison, DNA from the rape kits was tested, and Abbitt was ruled out as the perpetrator.

Michael Phillips' case is yet another in which perceived familiarity contributed to a wrongful conviction of an innocent person. In 1990, a teenage girl was assaulted by a man in her motel room. During the assault, she was able to pull up the man's mask. She said it was the man she had seen living at the motel, Michael Phillips (National Registry of Exonerations, 2017b). When presented with a lineup, the victim identified Phillips; he was later charged with the crime. His defense team suggested it was better to plead guilty rather than go to trial. He was sentenced to 12 years in prison and served the entire sentence. After a series of petitions, Phillips finally was able to get the DNA tested from the assault; it ruled Phillips out as the perpetrator. Unfortunately, not only had Phillips already served his entire sentence but also he had served an additional 6 months after failing to register as a sex offender for the sexual assault he never committed.

As the previously discussed real-life examples illustrate, a sense of familiarity with the perpetrator may be sufficient to lead an eyewitness to identify that "familiar" individual. Unfortunately, this sense of familiarity may or may not be accurate. In some cases, it is clear that a sense of familiarity resulted in misidentification and wrongful conviction. In other cases, the sense of familiarity was accurate in facilitating identification and conviction. Understanding the circumstances and factors under which each scenario may occur will help facilitate more just resolutions to crime.

Why Has Familiarity Been Ignored in the Eyewitness Literature for So Long?

To date, the "familiar-stranger" has received very little attention in the eyewitness literature. There are several possible reasons for this. Perhaps one of the main reasons for focusing on stranger identifications is the difficulty and "messiness" of manipulating and measuring familiarity, in addition to the numerous possible interactions that can occur with the notion of familiarity. Also, identification evidence often is the lynchpin that the criminal justice system relies on for prosecution and conviction of defendants. There may be a perception that identification from lineups is only necessary for "stranger-suspects." Hence, for approximately the past 100 years, research has focused on scenarios around stranger identification. As researchers move closer to approximate real-life situations to produce generalizable data, studying the construct of familiarity in an eyewitness context is critical for the next generation of eyewitness research.

Conclusion

The notion of a familiar-stranger, although less researched to date, is critical for understanding the reliability of eyewitness evidence. Studies have begun to investigate familiarity and its impact on the criminal justice system. When examining real-life crime, the majority of cases in the justice system appear to have witnesses with some familiarity to the perpetrator. Although we are a long way from understanding how familiarity influences eyewitness testimony, we hope this book will inspire a new domain of research that has at its core a notion of "familiarity" with the perpetrator. In the chapters that follow, we explore the current state of empirical psychological work on familiarity in an eyewitness context.

References

Bahrick, H. P., Bahrick, P. O., & Wittlinger, R. P. (1975). Fifty years of memory for names and faces: A cross-sectional approach. *Journal of Experimental Psychology: General*, *104*(1), 54–75.

Bornstein, B. H., Deffenbacher, K. A., Penrod, S. D., & McGorty, E. K. (2012). Effects of exposure time and cognitive operations on facial identification accuracy: A meta-analysis of two variables associated with initial memory strength. *Psychology, Crime and Law, 18*, 473–490. doi:10.1080/106831X.2010.508458

Clutterbuck, R., & Johnston, R. A. (2005). Demonstrating how unfamiliar faces become familiar using a face matching task. *European Journal of Cognitive Psychology, 17*(1), 97–116. doi:10.1080/09541440340000439

Flowe, H. R., Mehta, A., & Ebbesen, E. B. (2011). The role of eyewitness identification evidence in felony case dispositions. *Psychology, Public Policy, and Law, 17*, 140–159. doi:10.1097/a00121311

Greene, E., & Robinson, S. (1993). Who was that masked man? Demonstrative evidence in an eyewitness identification case. *Trial Diplomacy Journal, 16*, 249–252.

Gross, J., & Hayne, H. (1996). Eyewitness identification by 5- to 6-year-old children. *Law and Human Behavior, 20*, 359–373. doi:10.2307/1129636

Gross, S. R., Jacoby, K., Matheson, D. J., Montgomery, N., & Patil, S. (2005). Exonerations in the United States between 1989 through 2003. *Journal of Criminal Law and Criminology, 95*(2), 523–560.

Hinz, T., & Pezdek, K. (2001). The effect of exposure to multiple lineups on face identification accuracy. *Law and Human Behavior, 25*(2), 185–198.

Horry, R., Halford, P., Brewer, N., Milne, R., & Bull, R. (2014). Archival analyses of eyewitness identification test outcomes: What can they tell us about eyewitness memory? *Law and Human Behavior, 38*(1), 94–108. doi:10.1037/lhb0000060

Innocence Project. (2017a). *Clarence Elkins*. Retrieved October 12, 2017, from https://www.innocenceproject.org/cases/clarence-elkins

Innocence Project. (2017b). *Walter Snyder*. Retrieved October 12, 2017, from https://www.innocenceproject.org/cases/walter-snyder

Innocence Project. (2017c). *Johnny Williams*. Retrieved October 12, 2017, from https://www.innocenceproject.org/cases/johnny-williams

Memon, A., Hope, L., & Bull, R. (2003). Exposure duration: Effects on eyewitness accuracy and confidence. *British Journal of Psychology, 94*, 339–354.

Miethe, T. D., & Drass, K. A. (1999). Exploring the social context of instrumental and expressive homicides: An application of qualitative comparative analysis. *Journal of Quantitative Criminology, 15*(1), 1–21.

National Registry of Exonerations. (2017a). *Joseph Lamont Abbitt*. Retrieved November 4, 2017, from https://www.law.umich.edu/special/exoneration/Pages/casedetail.aspx?caseid=3807

National Registry of Exonerations. (2017b). *Michael Phillips*. Retrieved November 4, 2017, from https://www.law.umich.edu/special/exoneration/Pages/casedetail.aspx?caseid=4483

Pettalia, J. (2015). *Eyewitness identification of a "familiar stranger": The influence of personal knowledge and previous interaction on recall and recognition accuracy*. Unpublished doctoral dissertation, Carleton University, Ottawa, Ontario, Canada.

Pezdek, K., & Stolzenberg, S. (2014). Are individuals' familiarity judgments diagnostic of prior contact? *Psychology, Crime, & Law, 20*, 302–314. doi:10.1080/1068316X.2013.772181

Pozzulo, J. D. (2016). *Describing and identifying perpetrators: The young eyewitness*. Washington, DC: American Psychological Association.
Pozzulo, J. D., & Lindsay, R. C. L. (1998). Identification accuracy of children versus adults: A meta-analysis. *Law and Human Behavior, 22*, 549–570.
Shapiro, P. N., & Penrod, S. (1986). Meta-analysis of facial identification studies. *Psychological Bulletin, 100*(2), 139–156. doi:10.1037/0033-2909.100.2.139
Smart, E., Smart, L., & Morton, L. (2003). *Bringing Elizabeth home: A journey of faith and hope*. New York, NY: Doubleday.
State v. Williams, 146 Conn. App. 114, 116-17, 75 A.3d 668 (2013).
Steblay, N. K., Dietrich, H., Ryan, S., Raczynski, J., & James, K. (2011). Sequential lineup laps and eyewitness accuracy. *Law and Human Behavior, 35*(4), 262–274.
Vallano, J. P., & Winter, R. J. (2016). I think I've seen you before: How should courts deal with expert witness testimony when the eyewitness may have seen the perpetrator before the crime? *Judicial Notebook, 47*(5), 26.
Yarmey, A. D., Jacob, J., & Porter, A. (2002). Person recall in field settings. *Journal of Applied Social Psychology, 32*(11), 2354–2367.
Young, A. W., Hay, D. C., McWeeny, K. H., Flude, B. M., & Ellis, A. W. (1985). Matching familiar and unfamiliar faces on internal and external features. *Perception, 14*(6), 737–746. doi:10.1068/p140737

2

Theoretical Underpinnings

A Social Psychological Perspective

Early definitions of familiarity from social psychologists defined familiarity as the frequency of exposure to a person (Moreland & Zajonc, 1982). In addition, the duration for which we are exposed to a person is also thought of as becoming familiar with someone, especially as the duration increases (Mandler, 2008). Some researchers suggest that exposure duration can influence that "feeling of familiarity" (e.g., the number of times we see somebody) as well as the interaction between two people in terms of both quantity and quality. Marsden and Campbell (1984) suggested that a connection becomes stronger when the people in the relationship have known each other for a long time, communicate frequently, or feel emotionally attached. From a social psychological perspective, it can be speculated that both quantity (i.e., frequency of communication) and quality (emotional connection) play a role in familiarity.

Developing Familiarity

In order to become familiar with someone, researchers suggest that certain actions must occur prior to the development of familiarity. For example, the development of closeness and formation of relationships are two routes to familiarity. Aron, Melinat, Aron, Vallone, and Bator (1997) examined relationship development in pairs of individuals. Specifically, they examined whether closeness could be experimentally induced. In order to establish this closeness, they used self-disclosure and relationship-building tasks. Students were paired with one other student in their class whom they did not know. In

Familiarity and Conviction in the Criminal Justice System. Joanna Pozzulo, Emily Pica, and Chelsea Sheahan, Oxford University Press (2020). © Oxford University Press
DOI: 10.1093/oso/9780190874810.001.0001

order to do this, students first filled out questionnaires concerning their attitudes and attachment styles. After these questionnaires were answered, students were matched with one other student; however, participants could not be matched with someone whom they knew, and they could not be matched with someone who disagreed on any item that the other person rated as very important. The pairs then were given one of two different tasks to complete: a self-disclosure task whereby participants engaged in intimacy-associated behaviors with personal disclosure or a small-talk condition in which the tasks involved minimal disclosure. Upon completing the tasks, participants were given questionnaires to assess their perceived closeness with their partner. The results suggested that the type of task used to establish closeness is important, such that those who were in the self-disclosure/relationship-building group rated being closer to their partner compared to those in the minimal disclosure group. Interestingly, neither disagreement on important attitudes nor leading participants to believe they will like their partner influenced perceptions of closeness. Their third study examined whether closeness as an explicit task in which they were explicitly instructed to make a closeness goal (compared to implicit, in which they were not instructed to make this closeness goal) influenced feelings of closeness as well as being paired on the basis of extraversion (compared to introversion). Similar to Study 2, neither group reported more closeness than the other. Overall, Aron and colleagues' results suggest that closeness can be experimentally induced but more so when participants self-disclose with one another and engage in relationship-building tasks.

More recently, researchers have been examining two different paradigms with regard to determining what establishes and promotes familiarity. The first is the trait evaluation paradigm whereby people are asked to evaluate people they will never meet (Norton, Frost, & Ariely, 2007); the second is the live interaction paradigm whereby people interact in real time (Reis, Maniaci, Caprariello, Eastwick, & Finkel, 2011). The main finding from the trait literature is that the more information we have about people, the less we like them, perhaps due to the fact that having more information about another person poses more opportunity for dissimilarity. Norton and colleagues (2007) examined this notion across four studies, each with the same basic methodology. In Study 1, participants were presented with a survey regarding whether they would like a person more knowing "X" number of traits compared to "X" number of traits (e.g., two vs. four traits). In Study 2, participants were asked if they like people *more* the more they get to know about them. Both studies found that more information about a person results in more liking of that person; however, in Study 2, Norton and colleagues found that the more traits participants received about an individual, the less they liked that target individual. In Study 3, Norton and colleagues found that the relationship between number of traits and liking the individual less is mediated by the number of traits that were dissimilar between the participant and target individual. Last, Study 4 found that if a dissimilar trait was presented first, participants were less likely to find similar traits compared to when a similar trait was presented first. Although the participants never met these individuals whom they were rating, just knowing certain traits was enough to determine whether they would "like" them.

Reis and colleagues (2011) examined live interaction and whether familiarity promoted a liking or disliking of an individual. In their study, participants were asked to rate people they did not meet in person. Then, individuals who did not know each other were paired to discuss either two or six items to generate closeness. Participants were given a set of cards with questions, and one partner asked the questions and the other answered for 30 seconds. The roles were then reversed, and the first partner answered the same questions; this procedure continued until all questions had been asked and answered. Those who had the six different items of conversation reported a higher level of attraction, thus suggesting more conversation leads to more attraction.

Given advances in technology, familiarity also has been conceptualized as the number of instant messages and/or chats we receive from an unknown person (Reis et al., 2011, Study 2). As a follow-up to their first study, Reis and colleagues examined whether chatting online multiple times would increase attraction. Participants were given an anonymous screen name to log into an instant messaging client and were asked to chat for 10–15 minutes for a specified number of times (one, two, four, six, or eight times). No guidelines on what to discuss were given. Results indicated that as the number of chats increased, so did the level of attraction. Interestingly, other variables related to familiarity also increased when the number of chats increased, such as perceived knowledge of the other individual. The results of these two studies suggest that when there are high levels of social interaction (i.e., an establishment of familiarity), familiarity promotes an increase in attraction (Reis et al., 2011).

Proximity also plays a role in the development of familiarity (Verbrugge, 1983) because the closer physically one is to another person, the more contact they will have together, and thus familiarity will be established. In addition, Zajonc (1968) suggested that increased exposure leads to increased liking for that stimulus which could, in turn, establish familiarity. Although proximity plays a role in getting people together, these individuals must actually be interested in developing a relationship to the particular person. Early researchers examined whether the proximity between people would play a role in whether familiarity, and thus friendship, was formed. For example, Festinger, Schacter, and Back (1950) examined whether the physical distance between houses in a housing project impacted whether residents would become friends. The majority of friendships (65%) were between residents who lived within the same block. More recent research, in a different setting, also found similar results. Back, Schmukle, and Egloff (2008) examined whether proximity and group assignment influenced attraction to an individual, and thus familiarity leading to friendship. Participants were students in an introductory psychology course who were randomly assigned seats. Three different proximity groups were created: neighboring seats, same row but not neighboring seats, and no perceivable physical relation to one another. One year later, friendship ratings were obtained from each individual in the course. Students who sat in neighboring seats, or in the same row, had higher initial attraction scores compared to those with no physical proximity. In addition, those who sat next to each other, or in the same row, reported higher friendship intensity 1 year later compared to those who had no physical proximity. Back and colleagues' results suggest that physical proximity, even in a classroom, is enough to establish familiarity between individuals and thus lead to a friendship between them. We also are more likely to develop relationships with people who are positive and provide pleasant experiences. Berndt (1999) suggested that the stability of friendship is based, in part, on the positive qualities and interactions between the individuals, especially in children. This suggests that the more positive interactions we have with another individual, the more we will want to be around that person, thus leading to a heightened sense of familiarity.

Relatedly, the *mere exposure effect* suggests that the more we are exposed to a person, the more familiar we feel. For example, Moreland and Beach (1992) investigated the mere exposure effect by having four female confederates attend different lectures. Although these women did not interact with any of the students, they did take notes. When the semester had finished, students in the lecture courses were asked to view photos of the different confederates and answer questions pertaining to their impressions of the women. Interestingly, the women who were seen the most gave more positive impressions to the students compared to those women who attended fewer classes. In addition, students believed that they would enjoy spending time with the more familiar women more so than the less familiar women. Moreland and Beach's demonstration provides support for the notion that the more exposure we have to a particular person, the more familiar we feel with him or her.

Moreland and Zajonc (1982) examined the influence of the number of exposures on perceived familiarity, similarity, and attraction. In their first experiment, participants were shown a photograph of a male once a week for 4 weeks; half of the participants saw the same photograph each week (repeated exposure), and the other half saw a different photograph each week (single exposure). Participants then answered a series of questions concerning their perceived similarity and attractiveness of the target photograph. Those who had multiple exposures to the target photograph rated the target more attractive and similar compared to those who were only exposed to the target once. A follow-up study was conducted that found that as perceived similarity increased, so did attraction and perceived familiarity with the target photograph. Moreland and Zajonc's first study provides evidence that familiarity, defined as the number of exposures, can lead to an increased attraction and perceived similarity of the individual (Figure 2.1).

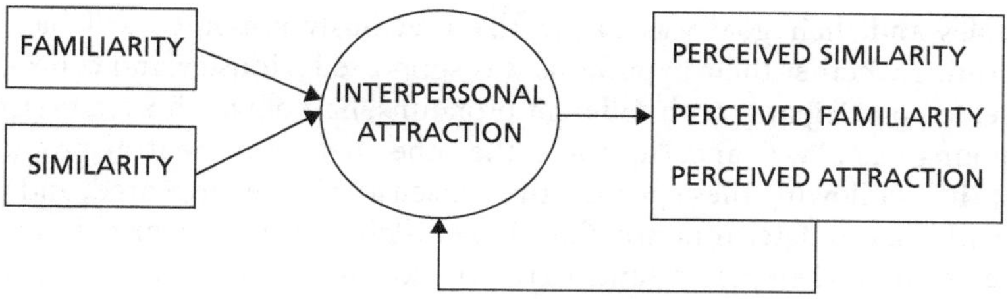

Figure 2.1 Exposure effects in person perception according to Moreland and Zajonc (1982).

Typically, individuals look for someone who is similar to themselves because similarity is another way in which closeness is established. For example, researchers suggest that demographic characteristics may be one influential factor in how people perceive similarity to others (Laumann, 1966). Reagans (2011) examined how social similarity and propinquity (i.e., being close to someone) play a role in strengthening connections among teachers. Data were obtained from teachers working in five different public schools who were given surveys four times during a 1½-year period to determine which factors (i.e., age, demographics, and proximity) influenced the social networks among these teachers. Both similarity and propinquity, individually and combined, were influential in determining how strong the ties were between individual teachers. For example, those who were similar in age were more likely to have a stronger connection compared to those dissimilar in age. This connection strengthened when the teachers were teaching on the same floor and thus had more opportunity to interact with one another; furthermore, Reagans found that the strongest network connections were among these same-aged teachers who taught on the same floor. Propinquity also played a role such that teachers who took breaks at the same time or taught on the same floor communicated more frequently and reported stronger ties. These results shed light on the fact that although similarity and propinquity can influence closeness individually, their combined influence creates a stronger connection between two individuals, thus leading to a higher degree of familiarity.

Another way in which familiarity may be triggered is through the use of inclusive pronouns (Housley, Claypool, Garcia-Marques, & Mackie, 2010). Housley and colleagues proposed that in-group pronouns may trigger feelings of familiarity given that positive stimuli are often perceived as familiar (Garcia-Marques, Mackie, Claypool, & Garcia-Marques, 2004). Specifically, they sought to determine whether stimuli are perceived more familiar if primed with in-group pronouns (e.g., "we") compared to neutral pronouns (e.g., "it"). Participants were informed that their long-term memory would be assessed through the recall of the capitals of all 50 states; the next task falsely informed participants they were subliminally presented with nonsense syllables and their goal was to identify previously presented syllables. To determine whether their hypothesis was supported, Housley and colleagues presented participants with different pronouns, half of which were in-group pronouns (e.g., "we" and "us") and the other half were neutral pronouns (e.g., "it"). Following these primes, the nonsense syllables appeared, and participants had to determine whether these syllables were new or old. Results indicated that when participants were primed with in-group pronouns prior to viewing the nonsense syllables, they were identified as familiar more frequently than those primed with neutral pronouns, thus suggesting that in-group pronouns do trigger a greater sense of familiarity compared to non-group pronouns. A follow-up study was conducted that replicated Study 1, with a more obvious exposure to the pronouns such that participants were aware of the priming stimuli, whereas in Study 1 they were unaware.

As the previously discussed studies illustrate, familiarity can be established in a variety of ways. As familiarity increases, so do a number of other variables, including attraction and closeness. It is intriguing that familiarity can be established without face-to-face contact (e.g., via instant messaging and chat rooms).

Stereotypes and Familiarity

Stereotypes can be defined as widely held beliefs about members of a particular group and have long been studied by social psychologists (Hilton & von Hippel, 1996). When we examine the definition of stereotypes, we can understand how familiarity plays a role in the development and maintenance of stereotypes, and their application to the in-group or out-group.

Gender stereotypes are perhaps one of the longest standing stereotype domains that have been investigated (Eagly & Mladinic, 1989). Nadler, Berry, and Stockdale (2013) examined the influence of familiarity and sex-based stereotypes on impressions of male and female faculty members across psychology students (Study 1) and law students (Study 2). They studied whether there were any stereotypes concerning each gendered professor. Participants were undergraduate students, and familiarity was varied using photographs of professors they knew in the college (e.g., familiar) and professors they did not know (e.g., unfamiliar). Different gendered professors were used to determine whether gender role stereotypes would impact students' decisions regarding which professor with whom they would want to take a class. Based on previous research (e.g., Ridgeway, 2002), Nadler et al. predicted that male university professors would be labeled more competent, and even more so when they were familiar. Participants were given a packet of 12 photographs that included four familiar faces (two males and two females). Participants were asked to rate each photograph on the person's competence and whether they would want to take a class with that person. Overall, the researchers' hypothesis was supported because male professors were viewed more competent than female professors. In Study 1, male university professors were deemed more competent than familiar female faculty. However, unfamiliar female professors were viewed as more competent than unfamiliar male professors. In Study 2, the familiarity and competence findings reversed such that there was a more pro-male bias for unfamiliar professors and a pro-female bias for familiar professors. Interestingly, Nadler and colleagues concluded that for psychology students, familiarity actually increased sex bias against female faculty, whereas familiarity decreased sex bias among law students.

Repeated exposure to a stimulus can produce a subjective feeling of familiarity toward that stimulus (Smith et al., 2006). Smith and colleagues (Study 1) examined whether repeated exposure to information influenced stereotyping. Participants were presented with a series of male and female faces and were subsequently presented with 12 person descriptions accompanied by photographs. Half of these photographs were seen in the first task, and the other half were new. Descriptions included information to be inconsistent with the occupation stereotype; three traits were provided in addition to the description. Results indicated that familiarity led to more stereotypical ratings such that when the descriptions were paired with previously seen faces, participants were more likely to rate those photographs as stereotypical compared to when new photographs were shown. Smith and colleagues concluded that perceived familiarity with a stimulus can increase the frequency of stereotyping that stimulus. Smith and colleagues conducted a second study with an additional question for half of the participants that asked about their subjective familiarity of each person description prior to giving their trait ratings. As expected, participants were more likely to rate previously seen targets as more familiar compared to novel targets. Similar to Study 1, the repeated targets were rated more stereotypically than the novel targets. However, this effect was weakened when participants were asked to consciously rate their subjective familiarity. This suggests that making familiarity salient to participants can make them conscious of their stereotyping, thus reducing the stereotyping.

In another study, Häfner and Stapel (2009) examined whether familiarity influenced stereotypes. The methodology was similar to that of Smith and colleagues (2006), whereby participants were presented with 30 male faces in the learning phase, followed by the test phase in which half the photographs presented were previously seen in the learning phase and half were not. Descriptions also accompanied the photographs and included stereotypical, categorical behaviors of the occupation of the target person as well as individuating information that was counter-stereotypical (Häfner & Stapel, 2009). After reading the descriptions for the photographs, participants were asked to rate different traits regarding the occupational stereotype. Results indicated that when participants were presented with categorical information—that is, information concerning the occupation of the target individual—they were more likely to judge the face as stereotypical when the face was familiar. Häfner and Stapel's results support the notion that familiarity led to an increase in stereotyping when a stereotype was presented with the photograph; however, familiarity led to less stereotyping when no stereotype was present with the target photograph. To apply this to real-world instances, Häfner and Stapel explain it in terms of friends and strangers:

> Because stereotypes are not on top of people's minds when dealing with a friend, the familiarity triggered by friendship or love does not lead them to judge their friends or partners in a more stereotypical way. However, when stereotypes are on top of people's minds, be it because they are all that is activated when they are exposed to strangers about whom they do not know much more than their social identity ("She is German") or because stereotypes are particularly accessible (e.g., because they are used repetitively in an argument; "But she is German!")—then familiarity experiences may in fact increase the use of stereotypes. (p. 621)

Now that we have provided a brief discussion of the development of familiarity and the role of stereotypes, we turn our attention to how the social psychological phenomenon of familiarity relates to the legal system.

Familiarity Applied to the Legal System

It can be expected that individuals will be more familiar with people in their in-group. An in-group can be thought of as a group that an individual identifies with as being a member, whereas an out-group is a group that the individual does not identify with (Oakes, Haslam, Morrison, & Grace, 1995). Social psychologists have long held that there is an out-group homogeneity effect whereby people perceive out-groups as more homogeneous and in-groups as more heterogeneous (Oakes et al., 1995). Researchers suggest that this may be, in part, due to familiarity, whereby more familiarity leads to the ability to individuate members of the in-group. This has been evident when examining influences of eyewitness identification accuracy. For example, the cross-race effect is the phenomenon whereby eyewitnesses are more accurate in their identifications of members of their same race (i.e., in-group) compared to members of a different race (i.e., out-group; Meissner & Brigham, 2001). However, researchers also have found that the more contact a person has with members of the out-group, thus establishing familiarity, the more the cross-race effect is minimized (Pica, Warren, Ross, & Kehn, 2015). As noted previously, it may not just be the quantity of interactions but also the quality of interactions that influence accuracy; the more positive the interaction, the more accurate we are at identifying members of a different race (Bukach, Cottle, Ubiwa, & Miller, 2012). For example, Pica and colleagues found that as the quality of contact with members of a different race increased, other-race sensitivity was improved. However, this was only true for those participants who currently had other-race contact. Thus, the familiarity between people of different races may have to be current in order to moderate the effects of the cross-race effect. The cross-race effect is discussed further in Chapter 6.

Calvin Wayne Cunningham is one individual who has been affected by both the cross-race effect and a perceived familiarity that the victim thought she and Calvin shared. There was an attack in an apartment complex early in the morning in which the victim was Caucasian and the attacker was African American (Innocence Project, 2019). The victim stated that she believed she knew her attacker, the man who lived across the hall in the apartment complex, Calvin Cunningham. Although there was DNA evidence at the crime scene, it was not tested. Based in part on this eyewitness testimony, which already was influenced by the cross-race effect, Cunningham was charged and convicted of the crime, and he was sentenced to 20 years in prison. Thirty years later, the DNA was finally tested, and it excluded Harris as the perpetrator of the crime for which he was convicted.

Interestingly, familiarity has also been suggested to play a role in Stockholm syndrome—that is, the bonding that occurs between hostages and their captors (Bejerot, 1974). Exposure duration is one way in which this can be established. For example, as the number of days in captivity increases, hostages become more dependent on their captors. In Stockholm, a bank was taken over during a failed robbery, and the hostages were not rescued until 5 days later. During the 5 days that the hostages spent with their captors, a psychological alliance was created between the hostages and the captors, most likely as a survival strategy. Once the hostages were rescued, one woman became engaged to one of the captors, and another helped with legal expenses for another captor (Logan, 2017). Although many do not understand this, the deep emotional response of being held captive made these women completely dependent on the captors and may have indirectly created a sense of familiarity (and safety?) within them.

Probably one of the most well-known cases of Stockholm syndrome is that of Patty Hearst (Adorjan, Christensen, Kelly, & Pawluch, 2012). Hearst, the granddaughter of a well-known publisher, was kidnapped by an urban guerilla group. After she had been kidnapped, videos were issued in which she condemned her friends, family, and the police while simultaneously expressing sympathy for the group that kidnapped her. Approximately 2 months after the kidnapping, Hearst was photographed participating in an armed robbery of a bank. Approximately 1 year later, Hearst was arrested (Adorjan et al., 2012). Her defense lawyer referenced Stockholm syndrome as a reason why she appeared to be a willing participant; however, this was not enough to acquit her, and she was sentenced to 7 years in prison. Slightly less than 2 years into her sentence, President Jimmy Carter commuted her sentence due the fact he believed she acted under duress; in 2001, President Bill Clinton granted a full pardon (Adorjan et al., 2012).

Conclusion

Social psychology is just one subfield of psychology that discusses how familiarity is established. If a person is similar to, in close proximity with, and sees the person on a regular basis, it is likely that familiarity will be established between the two individuals. These relationships can then be influential in the legal system. More research is needed to understand how the social psychological aspect of familiarity influences all parties involved in the legal system and interacts with other legal factors.

References

Adorjan, M., Christensen, T., Kelly, B., & Pawluch, D. (2012). Stockholm syndrome as a vernacular resource. *Sociological Quarterly, 53*, 454–474.

Aron, A., Melinat, E., Aron, E., Vallone, R., & Bator, R. (1997). The experimental generation of interpersonal closeness: A procedure and preliminary findings. *Personality and Social Psychology Bulletin, 23*, 363–377. doi:10.1177/0146167297234003

Back, M., Schmukle, S., & Egloff, B. (2008). Becoming friends by chance. *Psychological Science, 19*, 439–440.

Bejerot, N. (1974). The six day war in Stockholm. *New Scientist, 61*, 486–487.

Berndt, T. (1999). Friendship quality and social development. *Current Directions in Psychological Science, 11*, 7–10.

Bukach, C., Cottle, J., Ubiwa, J., & Miller, J. (2012). Individuation experience predicts other-race effects in holistic processing for both Caucasian and Black participants. *Cognition, 123*, 319–324.

Eagly, A., & Mladinic, A. (1989). Gender stereotypes and attitudes toward women and men. *Personality and Social Psychology Bulletin, 15*, 543–558. doi:10.1177/0146167289154008

Festinger, L., Schacter, S., & Back, K. (1950). *Social pressures in informal groups: A study of human factors in housing*. New York, NY: Harper & Row.

Garcia-Marques, T., Mackie, D. M., Claypool, H. M., & Garcia-Marques, L. (2004). Positivity can cue familiarity. *Personality and Social Psychology Bulletin, 30*(5), 585–593. doi: 10.1177/0146167203262856

Häfner, M., & Stapel, D. (2009). Familiarity can increase (and decrease) stereotyping: Heuristic processing or enhanced knowledge usability? *Social Cognition, 27*, 615–622. doi:10.1521/soco.2009.27.4.615

Hilton, J., & von Hippel, W. (1996). Stereotypes. *Annual Review of Psychology, 47*, 237–271. doi:10.1146/annurev.psych.47.1.237

Housley, M., Claypool, H., Garcia-Marques, T., & Mackie, D. (2010). "We" are familiar but "it" is not: Ingroup pronouns trigger feelings of familiarity. *Journal of Experimental Social Psychology, 46*, 114–119. doi:10.1016/j.jesp.2009.01.011

Innocence Project. (2019). *Calvin Wayne Cunningham*. Retrieved January 22, 2019, from https://www.innocenceproject.org/cases/calvin-wayne-cunningham

Laumann, E. O. (1966). *Prestige and association in an urban community: An analysis of an urban stratification system*. Indianapolis, IN: Bobbs-Merrill.

Logan, M. H. (2017). *Stockholm syndrome: Held hostage by the one you love.* Retrieved January 22, 2019, from https://www.linkedin.com/pulse/stockholm-syndrome-held-hostage-one-you-love-matt-logan
Mandler, G. (2008). Familiarity breeds attempts: A critical review of dual-process theories of recognition. *Perspectives on Psychological Science, 3*, 390–399. doi:10.1111/j.1745-6924.2008.00087.x
Marsden, P., & Campbell, K. (1984). Measuring tie strength. *Social Forces, 63*, 482–501. doi:10.1093/sf/63.2.482
Meissner, C., & Brigham, J. (2001). Thirty years of investigating the own-race bias in memory for faces: A meta-analytic review. *Psychology, Public Policy, and Law, 67*, 3–35.
Moreland, R., & Beach, S. (1992). Exposure effects in the classroom: The development of affinity among students. *Journal of Experimental Social Psychology, 28*, 255–276. doi:10.1016/0022-1031(92)90055-0
Moreland, R., & Zajonc, R. (1982). Exposure effects in person perception: Familiarity, similarity, and attraction. *Journal of Experimental Social Psychology, 18*, 395–415. doi:10.1016/0022-1031(82)90062-2
Nadler, J., Berry, S., & Stockdale, M. (2013). Familiarity and sex based stereotypes on instant impressions of male and female faculty. *Social Psychology of Education, 16*, 517–539. doi:10.1007/s11218-013-9217-7
Norton, R., Frost, J., & Ariely, D. (2007). Less is more: The lure of ambiguity, or why familiarity breeds contempt. *Journal of Personality and Social Psychology, 92*, 97–105. doi:10.1037/0022-3514.92.1.97
Oakes, P., Haslam, A., Morrison, B., & Grace, D. (1995). Becoming an in-group: Reexamining the impact of familiarity on perceptions of group homogeneity. *Social Psychology Quarterly, 58*, 52–60.
Pica, E., Warren, A., Ross, D., & Kehn, A. (2015). Choosing your words and pictures wisely: When do individuation instructions reduce the cross-race effect? *Applied Cognitive Psychology, 29*, 360–368. doi:10.1002/acp.3112
Reagans, R. (2011). Close encounters: Analyzing how social similarity and propinquity contribute to strong network connections. *Organization Science, 22*, 835–849.
Reis, H., Maniaci, M., Caprariello, P., Eastwick, P., & Finkle, E. (2011). Familiarity does indeed promote attraction in live interaction. *Journal of Personality and Social Psychology, 101*, 557–570. doi:10.1037/a0022885
Ridgeway, C. L. (2002). Gender, status, and leadership. *Journal of Social Issues, 57*(4), 637–655. doi: https://doi.org/10.1111/0022-4537.00233
Smith, E., Miller, D., Maitner, A., Crump, S., Garcia-Marques, T., & Mackie, D. (2006). Familiarity can increase stereotyping. *Journal of Experimental Social Psychology, 42*, 471–478. doi:10.1016/j.jesp.2005.07.002
Verbrugge, L. (1983). A research note on adult friendship contact: A dyadic perspective. *Social Forces, 62*, 78–83.
Zajonc, R. B. (1968). Attitudinal effects of mere exposure. *Journal of Personality and Social Psychology, 9*, 1–27. doi:10.1037/h0025848

3

Theoretical Underpinnings

A Cognitive Psychological Perspective

Memory is composed of three stages: encoding, storage, and retrieval (Tulving, 1972). Many researchers have proposed that memory, and specifically retrieval, is composed of two distinct processes: recollection and familiarity (e.g., Jacoby, 1991; Mandler, 1980; Yonelinas, 2002). Recollection is thought to be a conscious, intentional form of remembering that requires context to remember, whereas familiarity is more of an automatic process without the conscious effort. As such, in terms of memory, familiarity does not require context recollection. Although the majority of research examining this dual-process theory has focused on general memory, this also can be applied to a legal context such that an eyewitness may refer to a perpetrator as familiar because he or she remembers seeing the perpetrator but cannot remember the context in which this person was seen. Researchers believe that recollection may be more associated with episodic memory (where information concerning "episodes" in one's life and temporal–spatial relations are stored; Tulving, 1972, p. 385), whereas familiarity may be more associated with semantic memory (memory for the use of knowledge; Tulving, 1972, p. 386) as individuals may be aware they have seen this person/information before but cannot consciously report any episodic information concerning when or where the information was encoded (Jacoby, 1991; Tulving, 1985).

Familiarity and Conviction in the Criminal Justice System. Joanna Pozzulo, Emily Pica, and Chelsea Sheahan, Oxford University Press (2020). © Oxford University Press
DOI: 10.1093/oso/9780190874810.001.0001

Cognitive Psychological Theories of Familiarity

Whittlesea and Williams (1998) observed that feelings of familiarity occur more often when we have met an individual only a few times or when our mind tricks us into believing that a complete stranger resembles someone whom we may know. Whittlesea and Williams (2001) developed and tested the discrepancy-attribution hypothesis, which posits that familiarity is produced by the perception of discrepancy such as seeing a stranger we believe we have seen before (Whittlesea & Williams, 2000), and the heuristic basis of "feelings of familiarity." For example, Whittlesea and Williams (2001, Experiment 1) presented participants with a list of natural words (e.g., "smile") in the learning phase. In the test phase, participants were presented with sentence stems with a new or old probe. The stems were consistent or predictive in nature. When the stems were predictive (e.g., "She cleaned the kitchen floor with a . . ."; Whittlesea & Williams, 2001, p. 15), an illusion of familiarity was created. Interestingly, this illusion of familiarity was found only when the participants were uncertain about the outcome. Although these experiments were conducted using words, the results can provide a basis for a cognitive approach to studying, and ultimately understanding, familiarity in a legal setting. Whittlesea and Williams (1998) demonstrated that an illusion of familiarity can be created by causing participants to experience a discrepancy that was not due to a prior experience (as cited in Whittlesea & Williams, 2001). This discrepancy can be thought of as believing we should perform one way when encountering a certain stimulus, and thus believing that our actual performance is a discrepancy in how we think we should be behaving. Consider, for example, the stem mentioned previously, "She cleaned the kitchen floor with a . . .". In the test phase, participants may be presented with "broom," "mop," "rag," "cloth," and so on. Although all of these are ways in which we can clean a kitchen floor, only one of these words was previously seen (broom). In addition, although broom was the previously seen word, individuals may actually clean their kitchen floor with a mop, thus causing the discrepancy between what was seen before (broom) and what individuals actually do (mop). Individuals then attribute this discrepancy to believing they have encountered this stimulus before, thus creating that perceived sense of familiarity.

Monin (2003) examined the warm-glow heuristic, whereby the positive valence of a stimulus increases the perceived familiarity with that stimulus. Although previous research has demonstrated that people associate familiarity with a stimulus when the stimulus is easily remembered and interpreted, Monin proposed that a person's affective reaction is also a cue that the stimulus is familiar; this was later labeled the "good-is-familiar" phenomenon. Monin discussed two possible explanations for this phenomenon: prototypicality and affect-based. The premise of the prototypical explanation is that attractive faces are typically prototypical, and prototypes seem familiar (Monin, 2003). Research has reliably demonstrated that attractive faces are prototypical (Halberstadt & Rhodes, 2000; Langlois & Roggman, 1990; Meyer, 1956); this in turn increases a sense of liking, thus leading to a sense of familiarity. The fluency heuristic (Jacoby & Dallas, 1981) is another way in which prototypes can influence the sense of familiarity, such that when we believe we have encountered a stimulus before, we are more easily able to process that stimulus even when we do not have a prior mental representation for that stimuli. These different explanations led Monin to test the warm-glow heuristic, whereby liking is taken as an indicator of prior exposure and, hence, familiarity.

Across five studies, Monin (2003) demonstrated that the positive valence of a stimulus actually increased its perceived familiarity, even when there was no prior exposure to the stimulus. The purpose of Study 1 was to lay the groundwork for the remaining studies and provide support for the notion that prototypicality is not sufficient in explaining the relationship between attractiveness and familiarity. Separate groups of participants were asked to rate the attractiveness, familiarity, unfamiliarity, smiles, maturity/immaturity, and distinctiveness of 80 faces. Monin then computed average scores for each face and found more support for the relationship between attractiveness and familiarity. These 80 faces were then used in the learning and test phases for Studies 2 and 3. Studies 1–3 found that attractive faces seemed more familiar than unattractive faces, even when the inherent prototypicality remained the same (Study 3). Study 4 examined whether this would hold true for stimuli other than faces, such as words. The methodology for Study 4 was similar to that for Studies 2 and 3, but instead of photos, words were used. Three different types of words were used: positive (e.g., "glory"), neutral (e.g., "stamp"), and negative (e.g., "crime"). These words were presented in the learning phase. In the test phase, participants were asked to determine whether words had been previously seen or never seen before. Similar to faces, valence also influenced perceived familiarity of words such that positive words seemed more familiar to participants compared to both neutral and negative words. Last, Study 5 examined whether ease of recognition influenced perceived familiarity and later recognition. The methodology employed was similar to that of Study 2. Three conditions were created to vary ease and accuracy: delay and no warning, which was identical to that used in Study 2; delay and warning, in which participants were told to remember the faces and a delay was in place between learning and test phase; and no delay but warning, in which participants were provided with the warning instructions but there was no delay between learning and test phases. Monin found that participants were more likely to rely on the warm-glow heuristic when they were uncertain as to whether they had seen a face before and less likely when they were sure they had seen the face before (e.g., when they were instructed to remember faces). The results of these studies suggest that both positivity and attractiveness can create a perceived sense of familiarity, even when we have not been exposed to a stimulus prior to the recognition event.

Face Processing and Face Recognition

Before discussing the recognition/identification of a "familiar face" from a cognitive perspective, we present a brief description of face processing. A face must be processed before it can be recognized accurately. It is possible for errors to occur such that a face is recognized incorrectly as familiar. A false sense of familiarity is induced upon seeing the face for the first time. For the following discussion, we assume that a face was seen previously and processed.

Face Processing

Faces can be processed in two different ways: via configural/holistic processing and via featural processing. Faces are said to be processed configurally when we process the relations among facial features. In contrast, faces are said to be processed featurally when we examine specific features of the face (e.g., eyebrows, nose, and lips; Farah, Wilson, Drain, & Tanaka, 1998). When trying to determine whether a face has been previously seen, researchers have found that featural processing is inferior to configural processing because trying to recall only specific features of a previously seen face is not as efficient when trying to determine whether it was previously seen (Farah et al., 1998).

Development

The processing and recognition of faces begin very early, with research suggesting that even infants are able to process, recognize, and discriminate between faces (Bushnell, Sai, & Mullin, 1989; Kelly et al., 2007). Specifically, it suggests that the processing of faces may be heritable and that we process faces differently compared to processing and recognizing other objects. In addition, research suggests that specific areas in the brain are responsible for the processing of faces (Kanwisher & Yovel, 2006). Moreover, the ability to recognize faces changes as we develop, and there are developmental differences in how children and adults recognize familiar faces. Ellis, Shepherd, and Davies (1979) suggested that adults rely on interior parts of the face (e.g., nose, eyes, and mouth) to recognize a familiar person. However, when identifying an unfamiliar face, research suggests that adults rely on both interior and exterior parts of the face (i.e., hair, shape of face, and ears). In contrast to adults, research by Campbell, Walker, and Baron-Cohen (1995) suggests that younger children rely on exterior parts of the face (i.e., hair, shape of face, and ears) when recognizing a familiar person until approximately age 9 years. Some research suggests that this developmental trend may coincide with the development of configural visuospatial skills (Carey, de Schonen, & Ellis, 1992), leading to an increase in a child's ability to identify numerous faces or the development of an expertise of facial recognition (i.e., children require experience with seeing a number of faces to gain expertise in facial recognition, and adults have gained this experience of seeing many faces; Campbell et al., 1995).

There is also a line of research that suggests young children (aged 5 and 6 years) rely strongly on interior facial features when recognizing a face (Newcombe & Lai, 1994, as cited in Campbell et al., 1995). For example, in a study conducted by Ge and colleagues (2008), children (aged 4, 8, 14 years) were shown photographs that depicted solely interior facial features or exterior facial features of their classmates. They found that children were more accurate at identifying and recognizing their peers when exposed to interior facial features. Ge and colleagues argued that children move from reliance of exterior to interior features when identifying individuals due to an increased exposure to faces. Increased exposure to faces prior to a memory task reduces the cognitive effort involved in processing the face. Thus, it is possible that when recalling a face, the reporting of interior person descriptors, compared to complex faces, may increase for children. This shift in reliance on different features of the face could be associated with the age-related differences in reporting. For example, whereas adults focus on both exterior and interior facial features when encoding and recognizing strangers' appearances, children may rely more on exterior than interior facial features, which may result in children having less detail to report than adults.

Mondloch, Le Grand, and Maurer (2002) conducted a study examining developmental differences in facial processing. Participants—adults and children aged 6, 8, and 10 years—were presented with altered faces (e.g., inverted, and changes in shape and features), and it was found that face processing skills (i.e., accuracy in discriminating faces) improved with age. Specifically, children aged 6 years performed with improved accuracy when identifying simple changes related to features of faces (i.e., changes in lips, eyes, or mouth). However, children performed with reduced accuracy when identifying more complex changes in the faces (i.e., spacing of features and contour of features), whereas adults performed with much higher accuracy. Similar research by Schwarzer (2000) found that children do not perceive faces as well as adults because children rely more on featural processing (i.e., focus on specific features), whereas adults rely more on configural processing (i.e., focus on the face holistically). These studies suggest that when processing faces, "younger" witnesses may rely on more individual features, whereas "older" witnesses may process features as well as the relations between those features.

Face Recognition

In order to understand the role that familiarity plays in eyewitness identification specifically, it is important to first consider the role that familiarity plays in face recognition generally. Understanding how familiarity impacts our ability to process and recognize a face is a vital first step in understanding how familiarity may increase (or decrease) an eyewitness' ability to correctly make an identification from a lineup.

Eyewitness research studies employ a specific paradigm to examine factors that impact eyewitness accuracy. Most eyewitness research studies begin by exposing an individual to a target (i.e., perpetrator) through either a live, staged crime event or a videotaped mock crime. After a brief delay, the eyewitness is then asked to describe the target and make an identification from a photographic or video lineup. In most cases, the eyewitness is unaware that he or she will be witnessing a crime and also that he or she will be asked to identify the target from a lineup. This study method is employed in order to mirror the justice process as closely as possible. Despite this process, there is limited research available in which eyewitnesses are asked to identify someone with whom they are familiar. As mentioned in previous chapters, familiarity between an eyewitness and a target (perpetrator) can range on a continuum from completely unfamiliar (i.e., a stranger) to extremely familiar (i.e., a person with whom one has a close personal relationship, such as a family member; Pezdek & Stolzenberg, 2014). Despite the fact that eyewitnesses in the real world are often asked to identify someone with whom they are familiar (Flowe, Mehta, & Ebbesen, 2011), the majority of eyewitness research focuses on the identification of targets who are strangers (i.e., the eyewitness has never been exposed to the target before the commission of the crime). Due to this discrepancy between real-world identifications and eyewitness research, it is vital to begin to understand the role that familiarity plays in recognition by examining familiarity in the face processing literature.

Face recognition research employs a specific paradigm that is different from that used by eyewitness researchers described previously. Specifically, face recognition studies often test face recognition in two phases: exposure and recognition. In the exposure phase, participants are shown a series of photographs of novel (i.e., never before seen) faces. Later in the recognition phase, participants are shown another set of photographs, which contain some photographs of faces from the exposure phase along with a number of novel faces. In the recognition phase, participants are asked to determine whether each face is new (i.e., never seen before) or old (i.e., previously seen/familiar).

Differences in methods used by eyewitness researchers examining identification accuracy and cognitive researchers examining face recognition accuracy may or may not lead to similar conclusions. When considering the identification or recognition of unknown faces, accuracy rates differ between the two types of studies (Searcy, Bartlett, & Memon, 1999). Examining familiarity and its impact on accuracy also may lead to differing conclusions depending on whether one is examining the eyewitness literature or the cognitive literature. We discuss this further in later chapters. Here, we explore how familiarity is manipulated in traditional face recognition studies and the findings of this research.

Face Recognition and Familiarity: Exposure Duration

As mentioned in Chapter 2, exposure to a person or stimulus can create a sense of familiarity (Mandler, 2008). In addition to the number of prior exposures, exposure duration also has been found to be influential in creating a sense of familiarity in face recognition studies, such that the longer a person is exposed to another person, the more familiar he or she may feel toward that person compared to someone else with whom the person has had a shorter exposure.

As mentioned previously, cognitive researchers test familiarity by exposing participants to a number of faces and then ask participants to classify those faces as either familiar or unfamiliar. Bahrick, Bahrick, and Wittlinger (1975) conducted one of the first face recognition studies that specifically examined the role of familiarity in recognition. In this study, the researchers employed a cross-sectional design in which they tested participants' memory for faces of their high school classmates. Participants were asked to remember their high school classmates ranging from 3 months to 47 years after graduation. Participants were exposed to photographs from their high school yearbooks and were asked to recognize the people in the photographs, identify those people (i.e., provide their names), and match the names of their classmates to the appropriate photographs. Bahrick and colleagues found that participants were highly accurate at recognizing and identifying their former classmates, regardless of the time since graduation. For example, the mean accuracy of the face recognition task was 71% for those who had graduated decades earlier (i.e., 47 years since graduation). This study suggests that familiarity with a face increases one's ability to later recognize that face; however, methodological limitations of the study should be taken into consideration. Specifically, participants were exposed to photographed faces of their former classmates that were taken from the participants' own yearbooks—it is possible that participants had viewed their yearbooks and the photographs of their classmates from the time of their graduation to the study session. Furthermore, participants may have had exposure to their high school classmates after graduation, which would also impact their ability to correctly recognize familiar faces.

Vokey and Read (1988) employed a similar paradigm to study the role of familiarity and face typicality (i.e., distinctiveness) in face recognition. In this study, participants were again shown yearbook photographs and were later asked to (1) determine if a face had appeared previously in the sequence (i.e., make a recognition judgment), (2) determine the distinctiveness of the face (i.e., make a typicality judgment), and (3) determine if the face was "confusable" with someone they knew (i.e., make a familiarity judgment). The main purpose of this study was to determine whether familiarity played a role in false-positive responding (i.e., identifying someone as familiar when he or she has never been seen before). Intriguingly, Vokey and Read found no relationship between familiarity and false-positive responding.

More recently, Pezdek and Stolenberg (2014) employed a face recognition task to determine the role that familiarity plays in face recognition. The participants were sophomore students currently enrolled in high school. In this study, participants were exposed to 40 yearbook photographs of individuals who were either strangers (i.e., 20 unknown students who attended a different school) or casually familiar to the participants (i.e., 20 students who graduated from their high school 1 year previously). Overall, the researchers found that 42% of the casually familiar photographs were correctly rated as familiar, whereas substantially fewer stranger photographs were incorrectly classified as being familiar (i.e., 23%). These findings suggest that photographs of familiar individuals (i.e., past graduates of the high school) were significantly more likely to be rated as familiar compared to photographs of strangers.

Using meta-analytic techniques, Bornstein, Deffenbacher, Penrod, and McGorty (2012) examined face recognition studies ($K = 25$) and found evidence for a relationship between exposure duration and identification accuracy whereby the longer the exposure to a target, the more likely it was that the identification would be accurate. However, there was one caveat: The relationship was nonlinear such that exposure duration had the most influence when the exposure time was already short, thus suggesting that a longer exposure duration may not be as beneficial as once thought.

Recognition in the Real World

Although Bornstein and colleagues' (2012) meta-analysis was informative to the field, it relied on laboratory experiments. Valentine, Pickering, and Darling (2003) took a different approach to examine how exposure duration influences actual eyewitness identification and included 640 real-life cases in England between January and September 2000, resulting in 314 lineups. Horry, Memon, Wright, and Mine (2012) also took an archival approach and collected data from real-life cases between 1992 and 2000 in England. Cases were included if they had at least one lineup identification and the witness had no prior familiarity with the perpetrator. A total of 295 case files were examined, totaling 833 lineups. Eyewitnesses were only given one opportunity to view the lineup, the majority of which were live lineups. Approximately 30% of the identifications included eyewitnesses who had a short exposure to the perpetrator (less than 60 seconds) and approximately 70% had longer exposure (more than 60 seconds). Similar to Bornstein and colleagues, Valentine et al., as well as Horry and colleagues, found that when the exposure duration was more than 60 seconds, the rate of identifying the suspect was higher compared to when the exposure duration was less than 60 seconds. It is important to note that 60 seconds is a relatively brief period of time in real life, and some would argue that this time frame is not what is meant by "familiarity."

The results of both laboratory and field studies examining the influence of exposure duration on recognition suggest that the longer the exposure (up to a certain point), the more accurate the eyewitness will be. More research is needed to determine whether this longer exposure does, in fact, create a sense of familiarity to the perpetrator and what are the upper and lower limits of familiarity to influence recognition/identification. One such case is that of Patrick Brown. During a home invasion, the victim and assailants exchanged words and interacted with each other prior to the assailants leaving the house, thus increasing exposure duration. During the altercation, the victim was able to pull off the bandana from the face of one of the assailants; at this point, the victim believed he recognized the assailant as someone known in the neighborhood. Patrick Brown was misidentified in a lineup and spent 8 years in prison for a crime he did not commit because the eyewitness stated that he looked like someone he knew from the area (Innocence Project, 2018). Another case is that of Kirk Odom. A woman was attacked in her apartment and had minimal exposure to the perpetrator prior to being blindfolded (Innocence Project, 2019). Because she had minimal exposure, she was not sure she could positively identify her assailant. A composite sketch was created, and Odom was picked up after an officer thought he matched the sketch. When presented with a photo array, the victim selected Odom's picture but was not entirely certain it was him. She then was presented with a live lineup, during which she positively identified Odom as her attacker. Odom was charged and convicted of the crime, and he was sentenced to up to 66 years in prison. After spending 22 years in prison and 9 years on parole, he was finally exonerated of the crime (Innocence Project, 2019). These two real-life cases illustrate how both longer and shorter exposure duration to a perpetrator can be detrimental to eyewitness memory.

Face Familiarity: The Remember–Know–Guess Paradigm

Dual process theories of recognition posit that recollection and familiarity are two distinct processes. One way in which this theory has been tested is by using the remember–know–guess (RKG) paradigm (Gardiner, Java, & Richardson-Klavehn, 1996; Tulving, 1985). This paradigm has been examined across various stimuli, including musical melodies, words, and faces. For example, using melodies, Lange and Czernochowski (2013) examined whether timbre change would affect the episodic retrieval of novel melodies. Participants with "normal" hearing were presented with single-line melodies either twice in the same learning trial or eight times across four learning trials. In the test phase, participants were presented with a single melody and were asked to determine whether the melody was new or old (i.e., previously heard in the learning phase). If participants indicated the memory was old, they were then asked to indicate whether they "remembered," "knew," or "guessed" that it was old. Across three studies, Lange and Czernochowski found that a change in the timbre from learning to test phase influenced recognition. In Studies 1 and 2, results indicated that timbre change influenced both recollection and familiarity responses; however, the most detrimental change was for recollection. In addition, melodies that were presented in the same timbre were perceived as more familiar than those in different timbres. Similar to recollection and familiarity stemming from different forms of memory, many researchers believe that "remember" and "know" responses also may be associated with different forms of memory.

In a study by Gardiner, Ramponi, and Richardson-Klavehn (1998), participants provided explanations regarding whether they recognized a word because they "remember" seeing it before, "know" they have seen it before, or were just simply guessing that they had seen it before. Gardiner and colleagues found that participants who chose "remember" did so because they could recollect episodic information from when the word was encoded. Those who selected "know" reported that they had a *feeling* they had seen the word before; however, they could not place where they had seen it. Gardiner and colleagues' findings thus support the idea that "remember" responses may be more associated with recollection, whereas "know" responses may be more associated with familiarity. Gardiner, Ramponi, and Richardson-Klavehn (2002) further studied this issue by conducting a meta-analysis ($N = 23$) examining RKG responses. Results indicated that "remember" and "know" responses were associated with memory for the test item, whereas "guess" responses had no association with test item memory. These results suggest that the RKG paradigm can be best understood through dual process theories of recognition.

Although early research examining this paradigm focused on word recognition, some studies have examined it within an eyewitness identification paradigm and the results have been similar. For example, Meissner, Tredoux, Parker, and MacLin (2005) examined how lineup decisions were made using the RKG paradigm. Participants were exposed to multiple targets and asked to make an identification from a simultaneous or sequential lineup (for more on the sequential lineup, please see Lindsay & Wells, 1985), as well as indicate whether they "remember," "know," or "guess." Results indicated that when witnesses were presented with a sequential lineup, there was a reduction in "know" responses, whereas there was no reduction in "remember" responses, thus supporting the idea that the simultaneous lineup procedure promotes more of a familiarity-based decision.

To our knowledge, only one study has examined eyewitness familiarity with a perpetrator and participants' subsequent RKG responses. Sheahan and Pozzulo (2019) examined how familiarity influences eyewitness identification accuracy in an adolescent sample. Participants were high school students aged 15–17 years and were "more" familiar, "less" familiar, or strangers to the confederate. Familiarity was manipulated in such a way that during a group activity, the confederate worked directly with one group (more familiar) while the second group in the room worked without the confederate and only saw her (less familiar). Those in the stranger conditions never saw or interacted with the confederate prior to witnessing the crime. After a brief delay, participants were presented with a simultaneous, sequential, or elimination-plus lineup procedure. Most pertinent to this chapter is the RKG responses because the identification data are discussed in Chapter 4. When participants made a positive identification decision (i.e., selected someone from the lineup), they were asked to determine whether they made this selection because they remembered the confederate, knew the confederate, or were just simply guessing. Sheahan and Pozzulo defined "remember" as consciously remembering specific details about the face, "know" was defined as knowing they had seen the face before, and "guess" was defined as having no reason to believe the face was seen before. Eyewitnesses who were familiar with the confederate, and presented with a simultaneous lineup procedure, were more likely to indicate they made their positive identification because they "know" compared to when they were presented with a sequential and elimination-plus procedure (i.e., a simultaneous lineup with forced-choice decisions and confidence ratings) and the confederate was a stranger. Furthermore, when examining the rates of "remember" and "know" responses across familiarity, participants consistently provided more "know" or "remember" responses compared to "guess" responses when the perpetrator was familiar (more or less familiar) compared to a stranger (Sheahan & Pozzulo, 2019). Sheahan and Pozzulo posited that this may be due to the fact that when an eyewitness is exposed to a perpetrator prior to the commission of the crime, it establishes a sense of familiarity; thus, the eyewitness has a feeling of "knowing" he or she has seen the perpetrator before.

Face Recognition in a Legal Context

The research studies described in the previous section can be used as a basis to begin to understand how familiarity may impact eyewitness identification accuracy in the legal system. Although face recognition employs different research strategies to determine how familiarity impacts our ability to recognize previously seen faces, it provides some information regarding our ability to accurately determine whether a previously seen face is familiar to us. Face recognition research suggests that we are accurate at distinguishing between previously seen versus new faces.

Familiarity in a legal context is likely to be more complex than what is indicated in the face processing literature. The familiarity between the eyewitness and the [criminal] is one that is nominated by the eyewitness, such that the eyewitness will inform the police that the criminal is someone with whom he or she is familiar (e.g., a neighbor or a friend). This gives rise to the question: Can we trust that eyewitnesses are accurate when they claim to have seen or know the criminal before the commission of the crime?

One way in which cognitive psychology may help explain eyewitness identification with a familiar person is by use of the 10- to 12-second rule, whereby researchers posit that an accurate identification will be made 10 to 12 seconds after being presented with a lineup procedure. Dunning and Stern (1994) and Stern and Dunning (1994) believe this may be due to the fact that accurate positive identifications are more likely to be automatic, thus suggesting it may be, in part, due to familiarity with the criminal. Although this was not their objective, based on previous literature examining the automaticity of familiarity in recognition, it could be speculated that familiarity plays a role in fast recognition of a guilty suspect. Dunning and Stern examined how eyewitnesses came to their decisions when presented with an identification task. Across four studies, the researchers examined whether the decision processes varied between those who made accurate positive identifications and those who made inaccurate positive identifications. Results indicated that accurate identifications were made automatically—that is, no conscious effort in recollection was described—whereas when inaccurate identifications were made, witnesses reported a more deliberative decision-making process in which they used elimination strategies (Dunning & Stern, 1994). In addition, accurate eyewitnesses were quicker in their decision-making times. Dunning and Stern concluded that accurate recognition may be due to the automaticity of familiarity in recognition, whereas erroneous recognition may be due to the analytical retrieval process of recollection (Mandler, 1980).

Dunning and Perretta (2002) further examined the 10- to 12-second rule across four studies to determine whether accurate eyewitnesses made their decisions faster than did inaccurate eyewitnesses. All four studies employed similar methodology whereby participants watched a mock-crime video in which a man takes money out of a woman's wallet. Participants were then given a questionnaire to assess their recollection of the video and later presented with a lineup procedure to determine whether the perpetrator was or was not present. Last, participants were given a follow-up questionnaire on which they were to indicate their confidence and respond to questions concerning how they came to their identification decision. To measure reaction time, an experimenter timed the decisions from the videotaped recordings of the participants' identification decisions. The timing began when the experimenter put the lineup poster in front of the participant–witness and ended when the participant gave his or her identification decision. Across all studies, Dunning and Perretta found that eyewitnesses who were accurate in their identification decisions were more likely to make their identification within 10–12 seconds after being presented with the lineup. This suggests that familiarity may play a role because these decisions were automatic in nature, thus supporting the dual process theory of recognition, in which familiarity judgments are made quicker and automatically compared to when recollection is used.

Conclusion

This chapter examined various conceptualizations of familiarity from a cognitive psychological perspective. Intriguingly, familiarity has been operationalized and manipulated in the laboratory by cognitive psychologists, which does not square with more intuitive notions of what it means to be familiar. Does seeing someone for 60 seconds make that person familiar? Although one can argue that seeing a face for 60 seconds makes the person more familiar than seeing the face for 30 seconds, it is not clear that this has significant real-world value in the context of eyewitnessing. To truly understanding what it means to be "familiar" and its impact on identification most likely requires understanding from social psychology (see Chapter 2, this volume) as well as cognitive psychology.

References

Bahrick, H. P., Bahrick, P. O., & Wittlinger, R. P. (1975). Fifty years of memory for names and faces: A cross-sectional approach. *Journal of Experimental Psychology: General, 104*(1), 54–75.

Bornstein, B. H., Deffenbacher, K. A., Penrod, S. D., & McGorty, E. K. (2012). Effects of exposure time and cognitive operations on facial identification accuracy: A meta-analysis of two variables associated with initial memory strength. *Psychology, Crime and Law, 18*, 473–490. doi:10.1080/106831X.2010.508458

Bushnell, I. W. R., Sai, F., & Mullin, J. T. (1989). Neonatal recognition of the mother's face. *British Journal of Developmental Psychology, 7*, 3–15.

Campbell, R., Walker, J., & Baron-Cohen, S. (1995). The development of differential use of inner and outer features in familiar face identification. *Journal of Experimental Child Psychology, 59*, 196–210.

Carey, S., de Schonen, S., & Ellis, H. (1992). Becoming a face exert (and discussion). *Philosophical Transactions: Biological Sciences, 335*, 95–103.

Dunning, D., & Perretta, S. (2002). Automaticity and eyewitness accuracy: A 10- to 12-second rule for distinguishing accurate from inaccurate positive identifications. *Journal of Applied Psychology, 82*, 951–962.

Dunning, D., & Stern, L. (1994). Distinguishing accurate from inaccurate eyewitness identifications via inquires about decision processes. *Journal of Personality and Social Psychology, 67*, 818–835.

Ellis, H. D., Shepherd, J. W., & Davies, G. M. (1979). Identification of familiar and unfamiliar faces from internal and external features: Some implications for theories of face recognition. *Perception, 8*, 431–439.

Farah, M. J., Wilson, K. D., Drain, M., & Tanaka, J. N. (1998). What is "special" about face perception? *Psychological Review, 105*(3), 482–498. doi: http://dx.doi.org/10.1037/0033-295X.105.3.482

Flowe, H. R., Mehta, A., & Ebbesen, E. B. (2011). The role of eyewitness identification evidence in felony case dispositions. *Psychology, Public Policy, and Law, 17*, 140–159. doi:10.1097/a00121311

Gardiner, J. M., Java, R. I., & Richardson-Klavehn, A. (1996). How level of processing really influences awareness in recognition memory. *Canadian Journal of Experimental Psychology, 50*, 114–122.
Gardiner, J. M., Ramponi, C., & Richardson-Klavehn, A. (1998). Experiences of remembering, knowing, and guessing. *Consciousness and Cognition, 7*, 1–26.
Gardiner, J. M., Ramponi, C., & Richardson-Klavehn, A. (2002). Recognition memory and decision processes: A meta-analysis of remember, know, and guess responses. *Memory, 10*, 83–98. doi:10.1080/09658210143000281
Ge, L., Anzures, G., Wang, Z., Kelly, D., Pascalis, O., Quinn, P., . . . Lee, K. (2008). An inner face advantage in children's recognition of familiar peers. *Journal of Experimental Child Psychology, 101*, 124–136.
Halberstadt, J., & Rhodes, G. (2000). The attractiveness of nonface average: Implications for an evolutionary explanation of the attractiveness of average faces. *Psychological Science, 11*, 285–289.
Horry, R., Memon, A., Wright, D. B., & Mine, R. (2012). Predictors of eyewitness identification decisions from video lineups in England: A field study. *Law and Human Behavior, 36*, 257–265. doi:10.1037/h0093959.
Innocence Project. (2018). *Patrick Brown*. Retrieved December 12, 2018, from https://www.innocenceproject.org/cases/patrick-brown
Innocence Project. (2019). *Kirk Odom*. Retrieved January 21, 2019, from https://www.innocenceproject.org/cases/kirk-odom
Jacoby, L. L. (1991). A process dissociation framework: Separating automatic from intentional uses of memory. *Journal of Memory and Language, 30*, 513–541.
Jacoby, L. L., & Dallas, M. (1981). On the relationship between autobiographical memory and perceptual learning. *Journal of Experimental Psychology: General, 110*, 306–340.
Kanwisher, N., & Yovel, G. (2006). The fusiform face area: A cortical region specialized for the perception of faces. *Philosophical Transactions of the Royal Society, 361*, 2109–2128.
Kelly, D., Quinn, P., Slater, A., Lee, K., Ge, L., & Pascalis, O. (2007). The other-race effect develops during infancy: Evidence of perceptual narrowing. *Psychological Science, 18*, 1084–1089. doi:10.1111/j.14679280.2007.02029.x
Lange, K., & Czernochowski, D. (2013). Does this sound familiar? Effects of timbre change on episodic retrieval of novel memories. *Acta Psychologica, 143*, 136–145. doi:10.1016/actpsy.2013.03.003
Langlois, J., & Roggman, L. (1990). Attractive faces are only average. *Psychological Science, 1*, 115–121.
Lindsay, R. C. L., & Wells, G. L. (1985). Improving eyewitness identification from lineups: Simultaneous and sequential lineup presentation. *Journal of Applied Psychology, 70*, 556–564.
Mandler, G. (1980). Recognizing: The judgment of previous occurrence. *Psychological Review, 87*, 252–271.
Mandler, G. (2008). Familiarity breeds attempts: A critical review of dual-process theories of recognition. *Perspectives on Psychological Science, 3*, 390–399. doi:10.1111/j.1745-6924.2008.00087.x
Meissner, C. A., Tredoux, C. G., Parker, J. F., & MacLin, O. (2005). Eyewitness decisions in simultaneous and sequential lineups: A dual-process signal detection theory analysis. *Memory and Cognition, 33*, 783–792.

Meyer, L. B. (1956). *Emotion and meaning in music*. Chicago, IL: University of Chicago Press.
Mondloch, C., le Grand, R., & Maurer, D. (2002). Configural face processing develops more slowly than featural face processing. *Perception, 31*, 553–566.
Monin, B. (2003). The warm glow heuristic: When liking leads to familiarity. *Journal of Personality and Social Psychology, 85*, 1035–1048. doi:10.1037//0022-3514.85.6.1035
Newcombe, N., & Lai, L. (1994). *Young children's ability to recognize familiar and unfamiliar faces*. Unpublished manuscript.
Pezdek, K., & Stolzenberg, S. (2014). Are individuals' familiarity judgments diagnostic of prior contact? *Psychology, Crime, & Law, 20*, 302–314. doi:10.1080/1068316X.2013.772181
Schwarzer, G. (2000). Development of face processing: The effect of face inversion. *Child Development, 71*, 391–401.
Searcy, J., Bartlett, J., & Memon, A. (1999). Age differences in accuracy and choosing in eyewitness identification and face recognition. *Memory and Cognition, 27*, 538–552.
Sheahan, C. L., & Pozzulo, J. D. (2019). *"I know that guy!": Familiarity, lineup procedure, and the adolescent witness*. Unpublished manuscript.
Stern, L., & Dunning, D. (1994). Distinguishing accurate from inaccurate eyewitness identifications: A reality monitoring approach. In D. Ross, J. D., Read, & M. Toglia (Eds.), *Adult eyewitness testimony: Current trends in developments* (pp. 273–299). New York, NY: Cambridge University Press.
Tulving, E. (1972). Episodic and semantic memory. In E. Tulving & W. Donaldson (Eds.), *Organization of memory* (pp. 381–402). New York, NY: Academic Press.
Tulving, E. (1985). Memory and consciousness. *Canadian Psychology, 26*, 1–12.
Valentine, T., Pickering, A., & Darling, S. (2003). Characteristics of eyewitness identification that predict the outcome of real lineups. *Applied Cognitive Psychology, 17*, 969–993. doi:10.1002/acp.939
Vokey, J. R., & Read, J. D. (1988). Typicality, familiarity and the recognition of male and female faces. *Canadian Journal of Psychology, 42*(4), 489–495.
Whittlesea, B., & Williams, L. (1998). Why do strangers feel familiar, but friends don't? The unexpected basis of feelings of familiarity. *Acta Psychologica, 98*, 141–166.
Whittlesea, B., & Williams, L. (2000). The source of feelings of familiarity: The discrepancy-attribution hypothesis. *Journal of Experimental Psychology: Learning, Memory, and Cognition, 26*, 547–565.
Whittlesea, B., & Williams, L. (2001). The discrepancy-attribution hypothesis: I. The heuristic basis of feelings and familiarity. *Journal of Experimental Psychology: Learning Memory, and Cognition, 27*, 3–13. doi:10.1037//0278-7393.27.1.3
Yonelinas, A. P. (2002). The nature of recollection and familiarity: A review of 30 years of research. *Journal of Memory and Language, 46*, 441–517. doi:10.1006/jmla.2002.2864

4

Eyewitness Descriptions and Identifications of Familiar Perpetrators

Eyewitness evidence is often cited to be one of the most influential and critical pieces of evidence used in the justice system to investigate and prosecute defendants in criminal cases (Devenport, Penrod, & Cutler, 1997; Malpass & Devine, 1981; Wells, 1993; Wells & Olson, 2003). In fact, eyewitness evidence is one of the most common types of evidence presented in criminal trials (Devenport et al., 1997). Despite the frequent use of eyewitness evidence in the criminal justice system, eyewitness misidentification is the leading contributing cause of known wrongful convictions of innocent people (The Innocence Project, 2018). To combat this, significant research has been performed to exam the factors that may impact eyewitness memory with the hope to improve eyewitness recall and identification. The majority of this research has focused on an eyewitness' memory for a stranger, specifically a person who the eyewitness saw for the first time during the commission of the crime. Based on this research, a number of recommendations regarding the collection of eyewitness evidence have been established (National Academy of Sciences, 2014; Technical Working Group for Eyewitness Evidence, 1999, 2003). These recommendations are a set of best practices and guidelines that should be followed to ensure the reliability of eyewitness evidence.

Familiarity with a person has been found to impact people's ability to recognize a face (Pezdek & Stolzenberg, 2014); thus, familiarity is an important factor that may impact the accuracy of evidence provided by an eyewitness. Specifically, it is possible that familiarity may help—or hinder—an eyewitness' ability to recall details about a perpetrator and to make an accurate identification from a lineup (Petallia, 2015; Sheahan & Pozzulo, 2019).

Familiarity and Conviction in the Criminal Justice System. Joanna Pozzulo, Emily Pica, and Chelsea Sheahan, Oxford University Press (2020). © Oxford University Press
DOI: 10.1093/oso/9780190874810.001.0001

This chapter summarizes the available research that examines how familiarity impacts an eyewitness' description and identification of a perpetrator.

Role of an Eyewitness

An eyewitness can provide two types of evidence to investigators after witnessing a crime: descriptive information and identification evidence. *Descriptive information* refers to any information the eyewitness can verbally recall about the appearance of the perpetrator (e.g., "He had short, brown hair") or the events of the crime (e.g., "He was holding a knife" or "He ran out the front door"). Details regarding the appearance of the perpetrator are referred to as *person descriptors* and are used by police to narrow down the suspect pool during an investigation (Pozzulo, Dempsey, O'Neill, & Grech, 2009). Person descriptors also are used as a basis to choose fillers/foils (i.e., people who are known to be innocent of the crime in question) when creating a lineup in which to place the suspect (Luus & Wells, 1991). *Identification information* refers to the decision an eyewitness makes when presented with a criminal lineup. When viewing a lineup, the eyewitness must determine whether the perpetrator is present or absent from the lineup. Positive identification of a suspect may lead to an eventual arrest and prosecution, and identification evidence provided by eyewitnesses is often presented in court (Devenport et al., 1997).

As mentioned in Chapters 2 and 3, researchers often employ a specific paradigm to study eyewitness memory. In the common eyewitness paradigm, unsuspecting participants witness a mock crime. Then these participants, who are now eyewitnesses, are asked to recall everything they can remember about the appearance of the perpetrator and the events of the crime, usually in an open-ended format (e.g., "Tell me everything you can remember about the criminal"). Following a delay (ranging from minutes to days, months, or even years), eyewitnesses are shown a lineup (e.g., photo array) and asked to make an identification of the criminal.

When an eyewitness is shown a lineup, the lineup may be either a target-present or a target-absent lineup. In target-present lineups, the guilty suspect (i.e., the perpetrator) is included within the lineup, whereas in target-absent lineups the perpetrator is not present in the lineup and is instead replaced by an innocent suspect. Whereas the presence of the perpetrator can be experimentally manipulated in research studies, in the real world, police do not know if they are showing a witness a target-present or target-absent lineup (i.e., the police may erroneously apprehend an innocent suspect and place him or her in the lineup). When eyewitnesses are shown a target-present lineup, the only correct decision that can be made is a correct identification, in which the eyewitness selects the guilty suspect as the perpetrator. Incorrect decisions include the identification of a foil or filler (i.e., selecting a person known to be innocent by the police as the perpetrator) or a false rejection (i.e., stating the perpetrator is not present in the lineup when in fact he or she is). Alternatively, when shown a target-absent lineup, the only correct decision an eyewitness can make is a correct rejection. This occurs when the eyewitness states that the guilty perpetrator is not present in the lineup (i.e., the eyewitness does not make an identification). Incorrect decisions include a foil or filler identification, as described previously, and arguably the most serious error—a false identification. A false identification occurs when the eyewitness erroneously identifies an innocent suspect as the perpetrator.

As can be seen, there is potential for eyewitness error at either the description or the identification stage of an investigation. For example, the eyewitness could erroneously remember that the perpetrator had short, brown hair when in fact the perpetrator had long, black hair. This erroneous detail could lead police to search for an innocent person. Conversely, at the identification stage, the eyewitness could identify an innocent person, which may lead to the investigation, charge, and possible conviction of an innocent person, while the guilty person remains free.

Eyewitness Recall of Persons

The information that is recalled by an eyewitness can be extremely influential in regard to an investigation. For example, if an eyewitness describes the perpetrator as being "male, approximately 6 feet tall with brown hair," the police will use this evidence to begin to narrow down possible suspects. However, the descriptions provided by eyewitnesses tend to be vague in nature in that they can apply to many people (Lindsay, Martin, & Webber, 1994; van Koppen & Lochun, 1997). Consider the description just provided—a male, approximately 6 feet tall, with brown hair. This general description can apply to many people, which may limit the utility of the description during an investigation (Lindsay et al., 1994). Eyewitnesses also may leave out key information, such as the race or sex of the perpetrator. Lindsay and colleagues note that this may be due to what they call a "default value" rather than a lack of memory—specifically that eyewitnesses may not include information about race, for example, if the crime occurred in a racially homogeneous neighborhood. However, they note that eyewitnesses may leave out other key information, such as failing to mention the facial hair of the perpetrator or if he was clean shaven. This may be problematic when narrowing down the suspect pool or trying to determine appropriate foils for a lineup (Lindsay et al., 1994).

On average, eyewitnesses in laboratory studies recall approximately 7–9 person descriptors when they are asked to describe a perpetrator in a free recall format (Lindsay et al., 1994; Pozzulo & Warren, 2003). However, fewer details are generally recalled by real eyewitnesses (Lindsay et al., 1994), although descriptions provided tend to be accurate (van Koppen & Lochun, 1997). For example, Lindsay and colleagues examined the quantity and nature of person descriptors reported by 100 eyewitnesses in a sample of laboratory studies and real-world descriptions of 105 perpetrators published in a local newspaper. They found that on average, eyewitnesses to staged crimes (i.e., laboratory studies) provided 7.35 descriptors, whereas eyewitnesses to real crimes provided an average of only 3.94 person descriptors. When examining the type of descriptions provided by mock and real eyewitnesses, they found that eyewitnesses in laboratory conditions most frequently described the perpetrators' clothing, followed by hair color and height, whereas real eyewitnesses were more likely to indicate the sex of the perpetrator compared to mock eyewitnesses (Lindsay et al., 1994). Similarly, van Koppen and Lochun examined archival data from official court records that included 2,299 descriptions provided by 1,313 witnesses. They found that eyewitnesses cited the sex of the perpetrator most frequently, followed by height, age, appearance, race, skin color, and the presence of head coverings or disguises. Overall, it appears that eyewitnesses typically provide information that is vague (e.g., hair color) or easily altered (e.g., clothing). Although helpful, eyewitnesses often do not provide the most useful pieces of information that may give insight into the identity of the perpetrator (details that remain consistent over time, unique features, etc.) and help narrow down the suspect pool. For example, few real or mock eyewitnesses provide information regarding the interior facial features of a perpetrator (e.g., shape of eyes, nose, or mouth; Lindsay et al., 1994; Pozzulo & Warren, 2003).

Although informative, the research summarized thus far focuses primarily on the recall of stranger perpetrators. It is possible that familiarity may increase an eyewitness' ability to recall more information and possibly more accurate information about a perpetrator. Indeed, research suggests that familiarity with an individual increases our ability to learn and remember new details about that person (Kole & Healy, 2011). For example, across two experiments, Kole and Healy found that participants were more likely to remember fictitious details learned about friends and family members compared to strangers—a finding that was consistent even after a 1-week delay. Thus, it is possible that eyewitnesses may be able to provide more specific information regarding a perpetrator when the eyewitness and perpetrator are familiar—specifically, more details regarding interior facial features.

Petallia (2015) performed the only known study that directly examined the role of familiarity on eyewitness recall. In this study, Petallia manipulated familiarity between a confederate and participants whereby participants (1) interacted with a confederate and exchanged personal information with the confederate, (2) interacted with the confederate but did not exchange personal information, or (3) had no interaction with the confederate. The interaction between the confederate and the participant lasted approximately 15 minutes. After a delay of 5–10 days, participants were shown a video in which the confederate committed a crime. Following a brief delay, participants were asked to recall what they could remember about the criminal in a free recall format. Petallia found no association between familiarity and recall, such that witnesses provided a similar number of person descriptors, with similar accuracy, across all familiarity conditions. Given that Petallia performed the only known study that directly examined the role of familiarity on eyewitness recall, it is important to consider other areas of research that may provide more insight into how familiarity may impact recall accuracy.

Eyewitness Recall of Events

A significant amount of research has focused on memory for familiar environments and events. Research in this area suggests that familiarity may impact eyewitness memory through the activation of schemas. Schemas can be understood as cognitive structures that "help people anticipate, understand, and remember people, events, and settings" (Brimacombe, Jung, Garrioch, & Allison, 2003, p. 508). In the context of familiarity, schemas may work to assist eyewitness recollection of an event or environment by filling in any "gaps in memory" (Brimacombe et al., 2003, p. 509). Some research in this area has found that familiarity can work to increase the amount and accuracy of information recalled by an eyewitness. For example, Bruer and Pozzulo (2014) examined the effect of familiarity on children (aged 4–6 years) and adult eyewitnesses' ability to recall information about the environment in which an event occurred. The purpose of their study was to determine if being familiar with an environment impacted an eyewitness' ability to recall details about that environment. Participants were exposed to either child-familiar (e.g., a park) or child-unfamiliar (e.g., a bank) images for 7 seconds and were later asked to recall all they could remember about the images. Bruer and Pozzulo found that both children and adults provided significantly more details about familiar environments compared to unfamiliar environments. Specifically, they found that children were able to provide more details about the park image compared to the image of a bank, whereas adults provided more details when recalling the image of the bank compared to the park. Accuracy also was influenced by familiarity with the environment for the child participants, such that children were significantly less accurate than adults when they were recalling details about the bank; however, no differences in accuracy were found across age groups when recalling the park details (Bruer & Pozzulo, 2014). Overall, these findings suggest that familiarity may work to improve memory (both quantity and accuracy) when recalling environments in which an event occurred, especially for child witnesses.

Brimacombe and colleagues (2003, Experiment 1) also examined how familiarity with a crime environment impacted the ability of young adult, young senior, and older senior eyewitnesses to recall the crime. In their study, eyewitnesses were exposed to one of two crime videos in which a theft was either committed by a senior citizen in a seniors' activity center or committed by a young adult on a university campus. Brimacombe and colleagues (Experiment 1) hypothesized that familiarity with the environment would improve eyewitness accuracy—for example, young adults would have better memory for the theft on the university campus, and senior adults would have better memory for the theft that occurred in the seniors' activity center. Although no differences were found across familiarity for eyewitness recall accuracy, differences were found in the amount of detail provided by the older senior eyewitnesses, such that eyewitnesses spoke more words when describing the theft in the familiar compared to unfamiliar condition. However, Brimacombe et al. noted that older seniors in the familiarity conditions often described the conversations in the video, as well as off-topic speech, compared to younger eyewitnesses.

The impact of familiarity with an event has also been examined. Research examining memory for a repeated or familiar event has found that familiarity with an event can facilitate event memory through the use of scripts. Scripts (i.e., a type of schema) are typically developed when an event occurs repeatedly, and they work to provide a framework for understanding and remembering the event (Greenberg, Westcott, & Bailey, 1998). Specifically, when we repeatedly experience an event, we develop a set of actions or details that typically occur (e.g., at a birthday party, you eat cake). Scripts can be developed through personal experience or even through the media (Greenberg et al., 1998). Therefore, scripts may work to assist eyewitnesses in recalling event details if the event is familiar to them. For example, Ginet, Py, and Colomb (2014) found that witnesses were more likely to provide correct details after viewing a video about a woman participating in a surgical procedure if they were familiar with the surgical procedure (i.e., had a "surgical script") themselves compared to those who were unfamiliar with the surgical procedure (i.e., did not have a "surgical script").

However, exposure to a reoccurring or familiar event also may have a negative impact on memory recall. For example, although a script for a familiar event may help witnesses "fill in gaps" when their memory for an event is weak, this in turn may lead to errors (Greenberg et al., 1998). For example, Greenberg and colleagues (Study 2) examined participants' reliance on a crime event script when recalling a robbery in a convenience store. This study was conducted by showing participants a 24-slide sequence of a convenience store robbery in which either central details or peripheral details of the robbery were removed (e.g., the robber taking the money and the cashier removing money from the register, respectively). Participants viewed the sequence for either 2 or 8 seconds per slide and were tested on their memory for the sequence either 5 minutes or 1 week later (Greenberg et al., 1998, Study 2). The researchers found that witnesses were more likely to falsely recall details that did not occur in the sequence when the details were central to the script (e.g., robber took the money) compared to peripheral (e.g., cashier handed money), when they had shorter exposure to the slides (i.e., 2 seconds per slide), and when they were interviewed following a 1-week delay. These findings suggest that the use of scripts may negatively impact event memory and not always be helpful.

Familiarity with an event also may impact eyewitnesses when they are asked to recall a *specific instance* of an event that has occurred repeatedly. Research examining child and adult witnesses suggests that it is difficult to attribute specific event details to a specific event occurrence, which can lead to decreased accuracy in reporting compared to the reporting accuracy of those who experience a single event (Theunissen, Meyer, Memon, & Weinsheimer, 2017; Woiwod, Fitzgerald, Sheahan, Price, & Connolly, 2019). For example, Theunissen and colleagues examined recall accuracy of adult eyewitnesses who viewed either a single video of a distressing car accident or multiple videos of distressing car accidents. The participants who viewed multiple car accident videos were asked to recall only one target video during the interview. Theunissen and colleagues found that witnesses who viewed multiple videos were less accurate in their recall of the target event compared to those who viewed only one car accident video.

In summary, it appears that familiarity with a person or an event may work to increase or decrease accuracy in reporting. It is critical that we understand the parameters in which familiarity can be helpful versus harmful to an eyewitness' memory. More research is needed to explore real-life conditions as a function of perceived familiarity between the eyewitness/victim and the perpetrator.

Eyewitness Identification Studies

The identification of a perpetrator is typically determined through the use of a lineup task in which the investigator will ask an eyewitness to examine several photographs and make a decision regarding the presence of the perpetrator. Photographic lineups, also termed photo arrays, are used most frequently to identify a perpetrator due to their relative ease of administration in comparison to live or video lineups (Lindsay & Wells, 1985); however, live or video lineups are sometimes utilized (Humphries, Holliday, & Flowe, 2012; Pozzulo, 2016). A lineup is constructed of the suspect as well as a number of foils or "fillers." The suspect may or may not be guilty of the crime in question, whereas the foils are individuals who are known to be innocent of the crime in question and are typically "matched" to the description of the perpetrator that was provided by the witness (e.g., sex, ethnicity, and hair color; Luus & Wells, 1991).

Few research studies have specifically examined the role of familiarity on identification accuracy. However, the studies that have been conducted have generally found that familiarity increases the identification accuracy of eyewitnesses. For example, Petallia (2015) examined the role of familiarity on eyewitness identification accuracy. As described previously, Petallia manipulated familiarity by exposing participants to a confederate (mean time = 15.48 minutes) with whom they completed a task in which personal information was exchanged or no personal information was exchanged. A third group was never exposed to the confederate (control condition: stranger). Following a delay of 5–10 days, participants were exposed to a crime video in which the confederate committed a theft, and they were subsequently shown a target-present or target-absent lineup. Petallia found that eyewitnesses who interacted with the confederate were more likely to make a correct identification, regardless of whether personal information was exchanged, compared to the stranger condition (i.e., those who never interacted with the confederate). However, no differences were found across familiarity conditions with regard to the rate of correct rejections (Petallia, 2015).

Sheahan and Pozzulo (2019) examined the role of familiarity on adolescent eyewitness' (mean age = 16.54 years) identification accuracy. In their study, familiarity was operationalized by the type of exposure the eyewitness had to the perpetrator before the commission of a crime. Specifically, participants directly interacted with a confederate for 15 minutes (more familiar condition), spent 15 minutes in the same room as the confederate (less familiar condition), or had no exposure to the confederate (stranger condition). Following a delay, participants viewed a video in which the confederate committed a theft. Participants were then shown a target-present or target-absent lineup, and the type of lineup procedure used was varied. That is, eyewitnesses saw a simultaneous lineup (i.e., a lineup in which all photographs are shown at once), a sequential lineup (i.e., photographs are shown one at a time in a serial manner), or an elimination-plus lineup (i.e., a two-step judgment procedure). Similar to Petallia (2015), Sheahan and Pozzulo found that eyewitnesses were more likely to make a correct identification when they were familiar with the perpetrator compared to strangers, regardless of whether they interacted with or were simply exposed to the confederate for 15 minutes prior to the commission of the crime; however, this was only found when eyewitnesses were presented with a sequential procedure. Increased accuracy in identification decisions also was seen for witnesses who were presented with a target-absent lineup, such that eyewitnesses were more likely to make a correct rejection when they were familiar with the perpetrator compared to strangers. This increase in correct rejection rate was found when using the simultaneous and the elimination-plus procedures. Overall, the results of the previous studies indicate that identification accuracy of a familiar perpetrator interacts with other factors, such as the type of lineup procedure used.

In another study that did not directly manipulate familiarity, Steblay, Dietrich, Ryan, Raczynski, and James (2011, Experiment 1) examined the role of familiarity on eyewitness identification accuracy. In this study, familiarity was measured post hoc. Steblay et al. were interested in the influence of repeated viewing of the sequential lineup on identification accuracy. The confederate used in the study was a recent graduate of the college in which the experiment took place, with 35% of the participants indicating that they had some exposure to the confederate. They found that eyewitnesses were more likely to correctly identify the confederate during the first viewing of the sequential procedure when they were familiar witnesses compared to unfamiliar (60% vs. 7.6%, respectively). The increased accuracy of the familiar versus unfamiliar eyewitnesses also was maintained during the second viewing of the lineup (65.7% vs. 13.6%, respectively). Furthermore, familiar eyewitnesses were more likely to make a correct rejection of a lineup compared to unfamiliar witnesses on both the first (87.5% vs. 68%, respectfully) and the second viewing (68% vs. 45%, respectively). However, given that familiarity was not directly manipulated, the amount of prior exposure to the confederate was unknown (Steblay et al., 2011), limiting the applicability of the study.

Lucas and Brewer (2015) examined whether eyewitness identification accuracy was impacted when the perpetrator was associated with someone familiar to the eyewitness (e.g., "He looks like someone I know"). The researchers explained that the association with a familiar face refers to a specific characteristic of a perpetrator reminding the witness of a characteristic possessed by someone he or she knows (e.g., "He had my brother's eyes" or "His nose looked like George Clooney's nose"), leading to an association between the perpetrator and the familiar person. Lucas and Brewer noted that in these cases, familiar associations may be detrimental to eyewitness identification because the eyewitness' memory for the perpetrator may be altered by the familiar person during rehearsal. To test this, eyewitnesses viewed either a mock crime in which the perpetrator looked similar to a familiar famous person (e.g., Harry Potter or Paris Hilton) or a control video in which the perpetrator did not look like a famous person. After viewing the video, eyewitnesses were told to think about the appearance of the perpetrator over the time period of a week and then were asked to make an identification from a target-present or target-absent lineup (Lucas & Brewer, 2015). Overall, Lucas and Brewer found that although participants who made an association between the perpetrator and a familiar person thought about the appearance of the perpetrator more frequently over the delay (i.e., engaged in memory rehearsal), no differences in identification accuracy were found.

Last, other researchers have examined the influence of familiarity on child eyewitnesses. Cain, Baker-Ward, and Eaton (2005) tested preschoolers' recognition of familiar caregivers (i.e., caregivers who volunteered in their preschool for 6–8 weeks) by asking them to identify the caregivers from photographic lineups both 1 week and 3 months later. They found that children were able to recognize their caregivers with 28–75% accuracy, depending on the age of the child. Specifically, accuracy in recognition of caregivers was higher for older preschoolers compared to younger preschoolers and toddlers (75%, 41%, and 28%, respectively). This pattern was similar at a 3-month delay (Cain et al., 2005).

In summary, research examining familiarity in the context of eyewitness identification suggests that familiarity with a perpetrator can impact the accuracy of an eyewitness. However, given that familiarity is a broad construct that can encompass various definitions, and few studies have directly manipulated familiarity, no firm conclusions can be made. In order to gain a more comprehensive understanding of familiarity on identification accuracy, other areas of research need to be considered.

Consider a real-life example of familiarity. A witness was presented with a photo array and erroneously selected a man named Charles Chatman from the photos (Innocence Project, 2019). The case details involved a woman being awoken in her apartment when a male attacked her in her bedroom. Although she could provide a short description of her attacker, when she was presented with a target-absent photo lineup of six photographs the day after the attack, she did not identify any of the men. A second photo array was then presented to her, this time including Chatman, whom she identified as the perpetrator. It was at this time that the victim stated she thought she had seen Chatman in her neighborhood several times during previous years (Innocence Project, 2019); however, at the time of the attack, she did not mention having been slightly familiar with her perpetrator. Two weeks later, she was presented with a live-person lineup, including Chatman, thus providing a second identification of Chatman as the perpetrator. Chatman was charged, convicted, and sentenced to 99 years in prison. He served 27 years before he was exonerated based on DNA evidence recovered at the crime scene.

Conclusion

As discussed throughout this chapter, there is limited research examining the influence of familiarity on eyewitness recall and identification accuracy. This may be due to the fact that familiarity is subjective and difficult to define. Not surprisingly, there is no standard definition of what it means to be "familiar" with a perpetrator; familiarity may range from seeing a perpetrator briefly before the commission of the crime to the perpetrator being a friend (Pezdek & Stolzenberg, 2014; Pozzulo, 2016). Given the breadth in defining what it means to be familiar, and given that familiarity may be composed of varying components (exposure to a person, having personal knowledge about a person, etc.), it is difficult to pinpoint how familiarity may impact eyewitness memory. Moreover, other factors may interact with familiarity to influence description and identification accuracy. The current state of research suggests that familiarity may be an asset in some cases and a deficit in other cases. It is critical to delineate the conditions under which familiarity is versus is not helpful. Chapters 5 and 6 explore factors that may interact with familiarity to influence identification accuracy.

References

Brimacombe, C. A. E., Jung, S., Garrioch, L., & Allison, M. (2003). Perceptions of older adult eyewitnesses: Will you believe me when I'm 64? *Law and Human Behavior, 27,* 507–522.

Bruer, K. C., & Pozzulo, J. D. (2014). Familiarity and recall memory for environments: A comparison of children and adults. *Journal of Applied Developmental Psychology, 35,* 318–325. doi:10.1016.j.appdev.2014.05.002

Cain, W. J., Baker-Ward, L., & Eaton, K. L. (2005). A face in the crowd: The influences of familiarity and delay on preschoolers' recognition. *Psychology, Crime & Law, 11,* 315–327. doi:10.1080/10683160418331294835

Devenport, J. L., Penrod, S. D., & Cutler, B. L. (1997). Eyewitness identification evidence: Evaluating commonsense evaluations. *Psychology, Public Policy, and Law, 3,* 338–361. doi:10.1037/1076-8971.3.2-3.338

Ginet, M., Py, J., & Colomb, C. (2014). The differential effectiveness of the cognitive interview instructions for enhancing witnesses' memory of a familiar event. *Swiss Journal of Psychology, 73,* 25–34. doi:10.1024/1421–0185/a000118

Greenberg, M. S., Westcott, D. R., & Bailey, S. E. (1998). When believing is seeing: The effect of scripts on eyewitness memory. *Law and Human Behavior, 22,* 685–694. doi:10.1023/A:1025758807624

Humphries, J. E., Holliday, R. E., & Flowe, H. D. (2012). Faces in motion: Age-related changes in eyewitness identification performance in simultaneous, sequential, and elimination video lineups. *Applied Cognitive Psychology, 26,* 149–158. doi:10.1002/acp.1808

Innocence Project. (2018). *Eyewitness misidentification.* Retrieved December 1, 2018, from https://www.innocenceproject.org/causes/eyewitness-misidentification

Innocence Project. (2019). *Charles Chatman.* Retrieved January 19, 2019, from https://www.innocenceproject.org/cases/charles-chatman

Kole, J. A., & Healy, A. F. (2011). Memory for details about people: Familiarity, relatedness, and gender congruency. *Memory & Cognition, 39,* 637–648. doi:10.3758/s13421-010-0051-2

Lindsay, R. C. L., Martin, R., & Weber, L. (1994). Default values in eyewitness descriptions: A problem for the match-to-description lineup foil selection strategy. *Law and Human Behavior, 18,* 527–541.

Lindsay, R. C. L., & Wells, G. L. (1985). Improving eyewitness identification from lineups: Simultaneous and sequential lineup presentation. *Journal of Applied Psychology, 70,* 556–564.

Lucas, C. A., & Brewer, N. (2015). Eyewitness identification when "the perpetrator reminds me of someone I know." *Psychiatry, Psychology and Law, 22,* 49–59. doi:10.1080/13218719.2014.918082

Luus, C. A., & Wells, G. L. (1991). Eyewitness identification and the selection of distractors for lineups. *Law and Human Behavior, 15,* 43–57. doi:10.1007/BF01044829

Malpass, R. S., & Devine, P. G. (1981). Eyewitness identification: Lineup instructions and the absence of the offender. *Journal of Applied Psychology, 66,* 482–489.

National Academy of Sciences. (2014). *Identifying the culprit: Assessing eyewitness identification*. Washington, DC: National Academies Press.

Petallia, J. (2015). *Eyewitness identification of a "familiar stranger": The influence of personal knowledge and previous interaction on recall and recognition accuracy*. Unpublished doctoral dissertation, Carleton University, Ottawa, Ontario, Canada.

Pezdek, K., & Stolzenberg, S. (2014). Are individuals' familiarity judgments diagnostic of prior contact? *Psychology, Crime & Law, 20*, 302–314. doi:10.1080/1068316X.2013.772181

Pozzulo, J. D. (2016). *The young eyewitness—How well do children and adolescents describe and identify perpetrators*. Washington, DC: American Psychological Association.

Pozzulo, J. D., Dempsey, J. L., O'Neill, M., & Grech, D. (2009). The relationship between recalling a person and recognizing that person. *American Journal of Forensic Psychology, 27*, 19–35.

Pozzulo, J. D., & Warren, K. L. (2003). Descriptions and identifications of strangers by youth and adult witnesses. *Journal of Applied Psychology, 88*, 315–323. doi:10.1037/0021=9010.88.2.315

Sheahan, C. L., & Pozzulo, J. D. (2019). *"I know that guy!": Familiarity, lineup procedure, and the adolescent witness*. Unpublished manuscript.

Steblay, N. K., Dietrich, H. L., Ryan, S. L., Raczynski, J. L., & James, K. A. (2011). Sequential lineups laps and eyewitness accuracy. *Law and Human Behaviour, 35*, 262–274. doi:10.1007/s10979-010-9236-2

Technical Working Group for Eyewitness Evidence. (1999). *Eyewitness evidence: A guide for law enforcement*. National Institute of Justice, U.S. Department of Justice.

Technical Working Group for Eyewitness Evidence. (2003). *Eyewitness evidence: A trainer's manual for law enforcement*. Washington, DC: National Institute of Justice, US Department of Justice.

Theunissen, T. P. M., Meyer, T., Memon, A., & Weinsheimer, C. C. (2017). Adult eyewitness memory for single versus repeated traumatic events. *Applied Cognitive Psychology, 31*, 164–174. doi:10.1002/acp.3314

Van Koppen, P. J., & Lochun, S. K. (1997). Portraying perpetrators: The validity of offender descriptions by witnesses. *Law and Human Behavior, 21*, 661–685.

Wells, G. L. (1993). What do we know about eyewitness identification? *American Psychologist, 48*, 553–571.

Wells, G. L., & Olson, E. (2003). Eyewitness testimony. *Annual Review of Psychology, 54*, 277–597.

Woiwod, D. M., Fitzgerald, R. J., Sheahan, C. L., Price, H. L., & Connolly, D. A. (2019). A meta-analysis of differences in children's reports of single and repeated events. *Law and Human Behavior, 43*(1), 99–116. doi:10.1037/lhb0000312

5

Factors That Can Interact with Familiarity

System Variables

Wells (1978) developed a useful categorization for better understanding the variables that can influence decision-making in the eyewitness context. The variables were described as either estimator or system. *System variables* are those variables that are under the control of the criminal justice system and can be manipulated after the crime has occurred (e.g., interviewing protocols and lineup procedures), whereas *estimator variables* are those variables that occur at the time of the crime and cannot be changed (e.g., age of the witness and race of the defendant). A number of system and/or estimator variables can interact with "familiarity" of the perpetrator to influence a witness' recall and identification accuracy. Familiarity in itself can be categorized as an estimator variable. This chapter focuses on system variables and their interaction with familiarity. Chapter 6 focuses on estimator variables.

Interviewing Protocols: Recall Memory

A number of interviewing protocols are available for the police to use with eyewitnesses and/or victims, termed eyewitness–victim (EV). We make the assumption that EVs are willing to provide the most complete and accurate report of their memory to police. Hence, they are not reluctant witnesses, as may be potential suspects. Moreover, we assume that EVs have no motivation to lie or withhold information regarding their knowledge or memory of the crime/perpetrator.

At the core of many interviews, considered "best practices," is the notion of "free recall"—that is, EVs are given the opportunity to report everything

Familiarity and Conviction in the Criminal Justice System. Joanna Pozzulo, Emily Pica, and Chelsea Sheahan, Oxford University Press (2020). © Oxford University Press
DOI: 10.1093/oso/9780190874810.001.0001

they can remember about the crime and perpetrator, in their own words without interruption or interference from the interviewer. There are a number of "protocols" available with free recall as the foundation (e.g., the self-administered interview [Gabbert, Hope, & Fisher, 2009] and the step-wise interview [Yuille, Hunter, Joffe, & Zaparniuk, 1993]). The cognitive interview (CI) is perhaps the most widely used of the protocols available that is consistent with best practices for interviewing EVs and is used in various jurisdictions throughout the United States, Canada, United Kingdom, and Australia. The CI is an interview protocol based on the principles of memory storage and retrieval (Geiselman et al., 1984). Although this protocol has undergone a variety of revisions, its primary goal always has been to establish a set of guidelines that increase accurate information and decrease inaccurate information provided from EVs. The starting premise is that the EV is the expert and the interviewer needs to create a supportive environment for the EV to report everything he or she can remember. The enhanced cognitive interview (ECI; Fisher & Geiselman, 1992) focuses on the following:

Rapport building: An officer should spend time building rapport with the EV in order to make him or her feel comfortable and supported.

Supportive interviewer behavior: An EV's recall should not be interrupted, and pauses should be waited out by the interviewer.

Transfer of control: The EV should control the flow of the interview, where the interviewer acknowledges that the EV witnessed the crime and is the "expert."

Focused retrieval: The interviewer should use open-ended questions *after* the EV has completed his or her free recall.

Witness-compatible questioning: The interviewer should keep consistent his or her questioning with what the EV is reporting (rather than switch between topics).

The CI and ECI have been tested on a variety of populations and under various conditions. For example, Wright and Holliday (2007) conducted two studies in the United Kingdom with different-aged participants, including younger adults (aged 17–31 years), older adults (aged 60–74 years), and older-older adults (aged 75–95 years). Compared to a "structured" police interview (i.e., what police without specific training are recommended to do) done in the United Kingdom, the CI and ECI produced a greater number of accurate details for "Person," "Action," "Object," and "Surrounding" across each group of participants without an accompanying increase in erroneous information. The following is an example of coding: "A girl pushing a green bike across the car park" was coded as girl (person), pushed (action), green (object), bike (object), across car park (surrounding) (p. 26).

Recall Memory for Familiar People

Little research has been conducted examining interviewing protocols when interviewing a "familiar" perpetrator with adults; however, some work has examined children's abilities. In a study by Lepore and Sesco (1994), the ability of young children (aged 4–6 years) to recall information about a target interaction with a teaching assistant (TA) during an interview was examined. Some children were "familiar" with the TA, such that they interacted with the TA for 1½ hours prior to the target interaction, whereas other children were "unfamiliar" with the TA, such that they did not interact with the TA prior to the target interaction. Children were interviewed immediately and then 1 week after the interaction. Those in the familiar condition were more accurate during the second interview (i.e., 1 week later) compared to those in the unfamiliar group.

In a recent study, Cordón, Silberkleit, and Goodman (2016) examined children's free recall ability in conjunction with familiarity. Children, aged 4–5 and 7–9 years, were either "familiar" with the target, such that they engaged in age-appropriate activities with the target for two 3-hour sessions, or placed in the "unfamiliar" condition, engaging in the same activities but not with the target. Two weeks after the second 3-hour session, the interviews took place. Children were asked to identify photos of the target, and this was followed by an interview session. Although familiarity did not influence memory for the free recall, it did increase performance on closed-ended questions (Cordón et al., 2016). These results suggest that more exposure to a target leads to greater familiarity, which in turn leads to a higher proportion of correct responses when asked closed-ended questions. The results of the previously discussed studies suggest that increased interaction time with a target improves children's memory performance.

Recall from Chapter 1 that there are a number of real-life cases in which child EVs were "mistaken" in their sense of familiarity for the perpetrator. For example, Levon Brooks was wrongly identified by a 5-year-old witness, who told police that the man who abducted her sister in the middle of the night was her mother's ex-boyfriend. Brooks spent 16 years in prison for this crime, which he did not commit, and was only exonerated due to later testing of DNA evidence found at the crime scene (Innocence Project, 2019). Of course, sometimes children get it right, as in the case of Elizabeth Smart, whose sister Mary Elizabeth recognized the abductor's voice as one that was familiar—a male who briefly worked at the house.

Recall Memory for Familiar Environment and Event

Witnesses may not necessarily be familiar with the perpetrator, but they may be familiar with where the crime occurred. Ginet, Py, and Colomb (2014) examined whether various components of the CI would be useful for participants who are familiar versus those who are not familiar with a target event (i.e., surgical operation). Two free recall interviews took place. The first included the same instructions across all conditions, and the second interview examined one of the CI components. Specifically, Ginet and colleagues examined each of the four components of the CI individually to determine whether one component was superior to the others. Participants were divided into one of five groups: (1) context reinstatement; (2) report everything; (3) change temporal order; (4) change perspective; and (5) motivated instruction, which served as the control group. Across all components of the CI, being familiar with the target event elicited more accurate details than being unfamiliar with the event. However, two aspects of the CI seemed particularly useful in producing an increase in accurate information—namely "report everything" and "context reinstatement"—compared to using a "standard" free recall approach. Thus, the efficacy of the CI is extended when witnesses are asked to recall a familiar event. Moreover, knowledge of a particular "script" (i.e., protocol of what typically occurs) can be helpful when recalling events (Migueles & Garcia-Bajos, 2012; see also Chapter 4, this volume). These knowledge structures may aid memory by facilitating the organization of details. By having these knowledge structures already in place, a person's cognitive load (i.e., the amount of mental effort required for a task) is lessened and freed to focus on other details. It is important to note, however, that those familiar with a script also may produce more erroneous information, especially if it is inconsistent with the event (Migueles & Garcia-Bajos, 2012). The CI remains effective for interviewing witnesses who may be familiar with a particular event.

Also considering context familiarity, Bruer and Pozzulo (2014) examined whether familiarity with a specific place (i.e., a park or a bank) influenced recall accuracy among children (aged 4–6 years) and adults (aged 18–63 years). Participants were shown a series of images of a park (child-familiar) or bank (child-unfamiliar) and were later asked to orally recall what they remembered about the images. Children and adults reported more information when recalling an environment with which they were more familiar compared to the less familiar environment. Children reported significantly more descriptors for the park as opposed to the bank, and adults reported more descriptors for the bank as opposed to the park. Interestingly, although adults reported more information than children overall, when recalling the familiar environment, the number of descriptors and accuracy with those descriptors reported were comparable between children and adults.

Stereotypes

With familiar contexts may come familiar scripts or protocols as well as stereotypes (i.e., the perceptions, beliefs, and expectations a person has about members of a particular group; Dovidio & Gaertner, 2010). Cordón and colleagues (2016) examined how stereotypes, combined with familiarity, influenced recall abilities. In addition to the exposure to the target, children also were divided into a negative stereotype group or no stereotype group. Children in the negative stereotype group were read a story that depicted the target camp leader as a messy and clumsy person; those in the no stereotype group were not exposed to this information. When children were asked specific closed-ended questions about stereotype-related information (i.e., "Was Debbie messy or clean?"), their accuracy decreased. Familiarity and stereotypes interacted to influence overall correct responses such that children in the unfamiliar/stereotype-induced condition reported more accurate details compared to those in the unfamiliar/no-stereotype condition (Cordón et al., 2016). Stereotypes can lead us astray for familiar information when that information is inconsistent with the stereotype.

Leichtman and Ceci (1995) examined eyewitness memories in children aged 3–6 years. A man named Sam Stone visited the children; however, prior to the visit, children were assigned to one of four groups. The children in the control group received no information about Sam Stone. The children in the stereotype condition received information about Sam Stone's personality before his visit to the school. Children in the suggestion condition (i.e., implying a particular response) did not receive stereotype information prior to being exposed to Sam Stone, but they did receive a post-event manipulation that consisted of suggestive interviewing techniques. Last, children in the stereotype plus suggestion group were exposed to both the stereotype prior to being exposed to Sam Stone and the suggestive interviewing after the exposure. Sam Stone entered the classroom and said hello to the teacher and then was introduced to the children. He commented on the book that the teacher was reading to the children, walked around the classroom, and left. The exposure lasted approximately 2 minutes. The next day, the teacher showed the children a torn teddy bear (Leichtman & Ceci, 1995). Children were interviewed 10 weeks later. They were asked whether Sam Stone performed certain activities, such as damaging the teddy bear. Although the stereotyping did not have an effect on children's free recall abilities, it did affect their ability to accurately answer the probing questions. Children who were in the stereotype condition were more likely to state that Sam Stone was responsible for the torn teddy bear; some children even stated they saw him tear the teddy bear. Very few of the children who did not receive the stereotype prior to seeing Sam Stone made this same error.

Memon, Holliday, and Hill (2006) also examined whether pre-event stereotypes could influence children's memories. Children (mean age = 5 years, 9 months) were assigned to one of three stereotype conditions: negative stereotype (i.e., clumsy), positive stereotype (i.e., careful), and no stereotype. Children were then read a book about Jim Step and the activities in which he engaged. Jim Step visited the classroom for 15 minutes after the stories were read. After his visit, children were read a post-event narrative that contained both positive and negative misleading details about his visit. On the final day, children engaged in one last interview to determine whether stereotypes and post-narrative information influenced their free recall. Memon and colleagues found that the positive stereotype did influence children's recall when combined with positive post-event misinformation, such that the children in this condition were more likely to accept the positive misinformation compared to the children in the negative stereotype or no stereotype conditions.

In a study focused on adults, Kleider, Pezdek, Goldinger, and Kirk (2008, Study 1) examined whether schemas, or scripts, impact memories for events. Participants were told to study photographs depicting stereotype-consistent and stereotype-inconsistent actions by a handyman and homemaker. Following a 20-minute delay or 2 days later, participants were asked to determine whether different action statements were old or new. If participants selected "old," they were then asked which person performed the action and whether they remembered or knew that this was the person who performed the action. Hits (i.e., correctly stating the action was old) were higher in the immediate test phase compared to the delayed test phase. In addition, when tested immediately, stereotype-inconsistent actions were remembered better than stereotype-consistent actions. However, there were more source misattributions when the actions were performed by a stereotype-inconsistent actor (e.g., female handyman) than the stereotype-consistent actor. When participants indicated an action as "new," they were more likely to make attributions to the stereotype-consistent actor compared to the stereotype-inconsistent actor, suggesting that when participants falsely recalled these actions, they likely relied on stereotypes to determine the source (Kleider et al., 2008). These results suggest that memory for events does fade over time, and when memory is tested at a later date, a schema-consistent modification of memory is present. These schemas (or scripts) help fill in the blanks of what people expect to have happened.

A sense of familiarity toward a perpetrator, familiarity with the location where the crime occurred, and people's stereotypes can all interact to produce accurate and inaccurate details of the crime and perpetrator. Best practice interview protocols that avoid suggestive or misleading questioning are likely critical to avoid influences of familiarity that may not necessarily be accurate. Research should be pursued to validate the influence of good interviewing protocols when a sense of familiarity is suspected.

Lineup Identification: Recognition Memory

As mentioned elsewhere in this book, two scenarios can occur in real life: The police may have apprehended a guilty suspect or they may have apprehended an innocent suspect. These two scenarios have different consequences for the suspect as well as the larger community. A guilty suspect who is found guilty can be dealt with by the criminal justice system (through incarceration and/or other sanctions) to decrease the likelihood that he or she will commit further crime. If the suspect is innocent suspect, however, the person who committed the crime is still in the community at large and may commit further crime. Members of the community remain at risk for further crime to be perpetrated against them. Perhaps even more distressing, however, is that the innocent suspect may be convicted for a crime he or she did not commit. This conviction may mean serving time in prison and possibly experiencing other negative consequences. For example, even after an innocent person has served his or her time in prison, it may be very difficult to reintegrate back into the community. In addition, family and friends may be reluctant to provide support or associate with the innocent individual. An innocent ex-convict also may suffer further consequences when trying to rebuild his or her life because finding employment may be limited due to employers not willing to hire them, not willing to provide training, and so on.

Recall that in research, two types of lineups are created to simulate when the police have a guilty suspect (i.e., target-present lineup) versus when police have an innocent suspect (i.e., target-absent lineup). Target-present and -absent lineups allow us to understand the impact of different lineup procedures and other variables on identification accuracy. It is essential to consider the rate of correct identification of a guilty suspect as well as the rate of false identification of an innocent suspect that may occur with different lineup procedures, as well as other variables that may interact with identification accuracy.

Before discussing lineup procedures, we need to understand the possible decisions that can occur when a lineup is presented. With a target-present lineup (this would be the situation when the police have a guilty suspect), three possible decisions can occur. A witness can make a correct identification in which the EV identifies the perpetrator. Alternatively, the EV may identify a foil (i.e., a foil is a known innocent lineup member placed with the suspect), known as a foil identification. Last, with a target-present lineup, an EV may make a false rejection, in which the EV states the perpetrator is not present when in fact the perpetrator *is* present.

There are three possible lineup decisions when the police have an innocent suspect. With this target-absent lineup, the EV can accurately state that the perpetrator is not present in the lineup; this is known as a correct rejection. Similar to the target-present situation, the EV can identify a foil; this is a foil identification. Last, and most seriously, the witness may identify the innocent suspect as the perpetrator and make a false identification.

Both perpetrator-present (i.e., target-present) and perpetrator-absent (i.e., target-absent) scenarios can occur in real life. Of course, police have no way of knowing whether they have a guilty suspect (in which case a perpetrator-present lineup will occur) or an innocent suspect (in which case a perpetrator-absent lineup will occur). That is why EVs are critical to provide identification evidence. Theoretically, identification of the suspect increases the likelihood that the suspect is the perpetrator, and the non-identification of the suspect decreases the likelihood that the suspect is the perpetrator. Certain lineup procedures may facilitate more accurate identification evidence from EVs. Types of lineup procedures are discussed next, followed by a discussion on how a sense of familiarity with the perpetrator may interact with lineup procedure to influence identification accuracy.

Lineup Procedures

In the simultaneous lineup, the witness views all lineup members at the same time. This is perhaps the most widely used lineup procedure throughout the world (Wells, 1993). Witnesses viewing a simultaneous lineup may compare lineup members to each other and choose the member that looks *most* like the perpetrator, thus making a relative judgment. This strategy can be effective assuming the suspect is in fact guilty. Consider that a guilty suspect is more likely to look like him- or herself than anyone else in the lineup. Unfortunately, when the suspect is innocent, this strategy can be problematic and even dangerous, given that the most similar-looking lineup member is not in fact the perpetrator.

Lindsay and Wells (1985) developed the sequential lineup procedure to combat the reliance on a relative judgment. The sequential lineup presents lineup members one at a time to the EV. The EV cannot move forward (or backward) in the sequence unless he or she makes a determination of whether the lineup member being shown is in fact the perpetrator. It has been suggested that the EV compares his or her memory of the perpetrator with each lineup member, thus making an absolute judgment (Wells, 1993). Once the threshold of a "match" is met, the lineup member is identified.

The simultaneous and sequential lineup procedures have been compared across a number of studies as well as more comprehensively in meta-analyses. Steblay, Dysart, Fulero, and Lindsay (2001) conducted the first meta-analysis to compare the utility of the simultaneous and sequential lineup procedures. Support was found for the sequential-superiority effect, such that the sequential lineup resulted in higher rates of correct rejection in target-absent lineups and comparable rates of correct identification in target-present lineups after taking into account a number of real-world moderator variables. These results were supported in a meta-analysis conducted by Steblay, Dysart, and Wells (2011). Steblay and colleagues examined 72 tests of the sequential versus simultaneous lineup procedure. They again reported a sequential-superiority effect, such that the sequential lineup procedure resulted in fewer incorrect identifications when the target was absent from the lineup. However, they found that the simultaneous procedure resulted in more correct identifications when the target was present in the lineup. Steblay, Dysart, et al. (2011) maintain the superiority of the sequential lineup procedure given its higher diagnosticity ratio (i.e., rate of correct identification/rate of false identification) compared to the simultaneous procedure. A higher diagnosticity ratio suggests that decisions from that lineup are more indicative of guilt, thus suggesting that we can be more certain of guilt if an identification is made in the sequential lineup procedure compared to the simultaneous procedure.

Both the simultaneous and the sequential lineup procedures may pose challenges for younger aged witnesses, namely children. Pozzulo and Lindsay (1998) reported that the sequential procedure may exaggerate differences between child and adult eyewitnesses, whereby children produce even lower rates of identification accuracy and adults produce higher rates when using the sequential procedure compared to the simultaneous procedure. In an attempt to maximize children's identification accuracy, Pozzulo and Lindsay (1999) developed a lineup procedure known as the elimination lineup based on their two-judgment theory of identification accuracy, whereby witnesses engage a relative judgment followed by an absolute judgment. Witnesses who stop with a relative judgment or fail to make an absolute judgment are more likely to accept a lineup member as the perpetrator and make an identification. Pozzulo and Lindsay suggested that children are less likely to follow their relative judgment with an absolute judgment when shown a simultaneous lineup. To combat children's propensity to stop at a relative judgment, the elimination lineup requests two specific decisions. First, examining a simultaneous lineup, witnesses are asked to choose the person who looks most like the perpetrator. Once that decision is made, the remaining lineup members are removed and the second judgment is requested. Specifically, witnesses are asked whether the remaining lineup member—that is, the "survivor"—is in fact the perpetrator. This second judgment constitutes the identification decision.

Although the elimination procedure was designed specifically for child witnesses, it has been tested across a variety of ages (Humphries, Holliday, & Flowe, 2012; Pica & Pozzulo, 2017; Pozzulo, Dempsey, & Crescini, 2009; Pozzulo, Dempsey, & Pettalia, 2013; Pozzulo, Reed, Pettalia, & Dempsey, 2015; Sheahan, Pica, Pozzulo, & Nastasa, 2017). Overall, the elimination procedure produces comparable rates of correct identification and higher correct rejection rates for children compared to when the simultaneous lineup is shown (Pozzulo et al., 2009). For adolescents and adults, the elimination procedure seems to lower rates of correct identification and produce higher rates of correct rejection compared to the simultaneous lineup (Pozzulo et al., 2013; Sheahan et al., 2017).

In another identification procedure, known as a "showup," one photo is shown to the witness—that of the suspect. Because only one photo is presented, the procedure is considered highly suggestive—that is, the witness knows who the police suspect, and this knowledge may increase pressure on the EV to make an identification. Typically, showups are only permitted when a suspect is apprehended soon after the crime and near the crime scene. Alternatively, if police do not have enough time to assemble a complete lineup, possibly because a witness may die, a showup may be acceptable.

A crucial question is how, if at all, does familiarity or a sense of familiarity with a perpetrator interact with identification procedure. Although not manipulating lineup procedure per se, Lucas and Brewer (2015) were interested in determining whether a target who was rehearsed (or looked like someone familiar—that is, celebrity) would impact identification of the target using a simultaneous lineup. In their study, witnesses were either cued or not to pair the confederate with a celebrity. A target-present simultaneous lineup was used. Approximately 40% of participants made a connection between the confederate and the look-a-like celebrity. Making an association between the target and a famous person did not seem to influence identification rates. It is important to note that the association between the specific targets and celebrities used was not sufficiently strong to influence rates. Moreover, it is difficult to control the degree to which witnesses considered the cued associations.

Sheahan and Pozzulo (2019) varied lineup procedure (simultaneous, sequential, and elimination-plus) and degree of familiarity (more familiar, less familiar, and stranger) to examine whether the lineup procedure presented to eyewitnesses was influential when an adolescent eyewitness was familiar with the perpetrator (for a more in-depth explanation of the methodology, see Chapter 4, this volume). When participants were presented with a target-present, sequential lineup and were in the more familiar condition, participants had a higher rate of correct identification (.88) compared to both the less familiar (.68) and stranger (.58) conditions. No effects of familiarity were observed when participants were presented with a simultaneous or elimination-plus procedure. When participants were presented with a target-absent, simultaneous lineup and were in the more familiar condition, participants had a higher rate of correct rejection (.86) compared to both the less familiar (.61) and stranger (.52) conditions. Similar results were observed when examining the elimination-plus procedure such that participants were more likely to make a correct rejection when they were in the more familiar condition (.76) compared to both the less familiar (.54) and stranger (.35) conditions. Sheahan and Pozzulo's findings deviate from what is typically found with stranger identifications, whereby the simultaneous procedure elicits more correct identifications and the sequential procedure elicits more correct rejections. These findings suggest that being familiar with the perpetrator may in fact, interact with the lineup procedure and influences identification accuracy.

Because there are such limited data on lineup procedures as a function of "familiarity of the perpetrator," recommendations for best practices are not possible. It can be speculated, however, that lineup procedures encouraging the use of a relative judgment may be the most harmful to a "familiar suspect" given familiarity may lead the eyewitness to erroneously choose the person who looks most familiar, which in a target-absent procedure may be the innocent suspect. Whenever an EV reports being familiar or having a sense of familiarity with the perpetrator, it may be best to use lineup procedures encouraging absolute judgments so as to decrease the risk of false identification.

Measuring Confidence and Familiarity

One approach to obtaining identification evidence involves determining a witness' confidence level either prior to making an identification decision (e.g., "How sure are you that you can identify the perpetrator?") or after an identification decision has been made (e.g., "How sure are you that you made the correct identification decision?"). The rating is usually taken on a 100-point scale, ranging from "not at all confident" (1) to "absolutely confident" (100). The confidence measure is then used to predict the accuracy of the identification measure.

Although to date no studies have examined confidence and the familiar-stranger, some researchers have studied moderator effects (a moderator is a variable that affects the direction and/or strength of the relationship between two variables; Barron & Kenny, 1986). For example, Bothwell, Deffenbacher, and Brigham (1987) examined the confidence–accuracy relationship in a meta-analysis (k = 35) and also exposure duration as a potential moderator. The relation between the confidence–accuracy relationship and exposure duration produced a medium effect (r = .36). In addition, Read, Vokey, and Hammersley (1990) found that as exposure duration increases, the strength of the confidence–accuracy relationship also increases. These two studies examined the confidence–accuracy relationship with the point-biserial correlation.

Another option to assess the relationship between confidence and accuracy is to use a calibration approach that involves a continuous rating of confidence on a 1 to 100 scale and the plotting of the proportion of accurate identification responses across each level of confidence (Brewer & Wells, 2006). Researchers who use the calibration approach also have found support for the relation between the confidence–accuracy relationship and exposure duration. For example, Palmer, Brewer, Weber, and Nagesh (2013) examined whether exposure duration and the confidence–accuracy relationship were related and found that increased confidence was related to an increase in identification accuracy with increased exposure duration. However, an eyewitness' confidence in his or her identification was better able to discriminate between accurate and inaccurate eyewitnesses when exposure to the target was brief (i.e., 5 seconds). Carlson and colleagues (2016) also found support for this, such that increased exposure time resulted in better confidence calibration for choosers (i.e., participants making a selection) compared to non-choosers (i.e., participants not making a selection); however, this difference was not significant. It is reasonable to assume that a sense of familiarity would increase confidence, but this increase in confidence would not necessarily be predictive of identification accuracy.

Researchers in the facial recognition field have examined confidence and familiarity. For example, Bruce, Henderson, Newman, and Burton (2001, Experiment 1) examined whether participants could match identities of familiar and unfamiliar faces on closed-caption television (CCTV) images. Familiar faces in this study were academic staff from the university with whom the participants should have been familiar. Participants were shown moving clips, a single still image, or three different still images. Familiarity increased the number of correct responses compared to when participants were unfamiliar with the target. Moreover, participants who were in the familiar group exhibited higher confidence than those who were in the unfamiliar group.

Indices of confidence may prove to be useful when an EV has a sense of familiarity with the perpetrator. Further work is needed in this domain of "confidence" to understand the types of confidence measures (e.g., how and when confidence should be taken and what should be done with it once a confidence measure is obtained) that are most useful for identification of a "familiar" perpetrator. Perhaps a set of confidence measures can be used to determine whether a suspect is in fact the perpetrator.

A Case of Unconscious Transference: The Bystander Effect

A related concept to this discussion of familiarity with the perpetrator is unconscious transference or the phenomenon whereby someone near the perpetrator is misidentified as the perpetrator (Read, Tollestrup, Hammersley, McFadzen, & Christensen, 1990). A historically prominent case of unconscious transference that helped set the research of the unconscious transference/bystander effect in motion is that of the identification of an innocent sailor made by a train clerk. Wall (1965) discusses the events leading up to this erroneous identification. A train clerk who had been working at a train station for some time was held up at gun point. When presented with the lineup, the clerk chose a sailor, stating that the sailor was the man who held him up. The sailor was then taken into custody; however, he had an alibi that proved to be true. In subsequent interviews, the clerk stated that the sailor had looked very familiar to him. Further into the investigation, it was found that the sailor's base was near the train station, and the sailor had been to the train station on three different occasions to purchase tickets. The ticket agent mistakenly identified a familiar person as the perpetrator because seeing the photograph in the lineup triggered his memory of seeing the sailor at the ticket station, which is a classic example of unconscious transference. This case helped spark the interest of eyewitness identification researchers to determine why an innocent, but familiar, person would be chosen from a lineup.

Read, Tollestrup, et al. (1990, Experiment 5) examined under what conditions the unconscious transference effect occurs. Participants were undergraduate students who were attending a psychology class when the bystander entered the classroom and distributed graded examinations, distributed examination materials, notified the class that the instructor would be late, or was a disruptive tardy. The perpetrator, who posed as a technician repairing a faulty sound system, was observed by everyone in the classroom; he was in full view for 4 or 5 minutes. In the transference-before condition, a group of students saw the bystander 2 weeks before the perpetrator. In the same-day transference group, the students saw the bystander and the perpetrator on the same day, and in the transference-after group, the students saw the perpetrator 1 week after seeing the bystander. A control group was used in which the participants had no opportunity to observe the bystander. Participants received two lineup tasks: target-absent and target-present with low- or high-similarity foils. The unconscious transference effect was more profound in the low-similarity foil, target-absent lineup, with those in the transference condition misidentifying the innocent bystander at a rate of .25 and those in the control condition misidentifying the bystander at a rate of .12. In high-similarity lineups, both the transference conditions and the control condition performed comparably (.16 and .12, respectively).

Ross, Ceci, Dunning, and Toglia (1994) further examined the bystander effect across four studies that all employed a similar methodology. Participants watched one of two videos: The control group watched a video in which an innocent bystander was not seen, and the transference group watched a video in which an innocent bystander was observed. Participants were then presented with a target-present or bystander-present (i.e., target-absent) lineup procedure. In Study 1, when presented with the bystander-present lineup, participants in the transference condition were more likely to misidentify the innocent bystander (.61) compared to those in the control group (.20). In the target-present lineup, the transference and control conditions did not differ in their ability to make a correct identification. Studies 2–4 found similar results; however, in Study 2, the effect was eliminated when participants in the transference condition were informed that the bystander and perpetrator were not the same person (Ross et al., 1994). Studies 3 and 4 probed further and found that participants were making the mistake of misidentifying the bystander because they believed that the bystander and perpetrator were the same person.

Ross et al. (2006) examined whether the unconscious transference effect is present in children aged 5–12 years. Similar to the study by Ross et al. (1994), participants were randomly assigned to either the transference or the control condition, and depending on which control they were in, they viewed either the bystander- or the victim-present videotaped mock crime. Interestingly, the unconscious transference effect was only evident for children aged 11 and 12 years. This age group was significantly more likely to misidentify the bystander compared to the control groups and the younger age groups, suggesting that the advancement of cognitive abilities as people age may cause them to be more prone to making this error. In the target-present lineup, this age group was the most accurate in the identification of the thief.

Recently, researchers have suggested that "change blindness," whereby people fail to detect substitutions of one person for another in social interactions (Simons & Levins, 1998), may contribute to misidentifications. Davis,

Loftus, Vanous, and Cucciare (2008, Study 1) examined this phenomenon through a vignette depicting the shoplifting of a bottle of wine in a supermarket. Two innocent bystanders were presented: the continuous innocent (CI) and discontinuous innocent (DI). The CI person walked down an aisle and passed behind a tall stack of napkins, from which the perpetrator then emerged, walking down the aisle in a continuous motion prior to stealing the bottle of wine. The camera then switched views to the produce aisle, where the DI person was shown walking into view, grabbing fruit, and walking out of view. After viewing the vignette, participants were presented with a target-absent lineup that included the three confederates and three foils, with each of the three foils looking similar to one of the confederates. The majority of participants (.73) misidentified an innocent person. Interestingly, most participants did not notice the change between the CI and the perpetrator; moreover, these participants were more likely to misidentify the CI than the DI (.41 and .23, respectively). Davis and colleagues conducted a follow-up study with similar methodology as that of their first study, but Study 2 also included a distraction in which half of the participants were asked to memorize at least two products per aisle, whereas the other half of participants were not. Similar results as those obtained in Study 1 were found such that those who did not notice the change between the CI and the perpetrator were more likely to misidentify the CI as the perpetrator compared to the DI (.42 and .24, respectively). This significance disappeared when the distraction was introduced. Finally, Davis and colleagues conducted a third study that included separate lineups for the CI and the DI. Again, they were more likely to misidentify the CI (.34) compared to the DI (.15), even when the CI and the DI were presented in individual lineups. The results of these studies suggest that shallow processing, thus creating a sense of familiarity, may be an underlying process that aids in the erroneous identification of innocent bystanders to crime.

Commitment Effect

Some research has found that once someone is seen previously, such as in a mugshot search, he or she becomes "familiar," thus increasing the likelihood that he or she will be identified in a lineup (Loftus, 1976). This phenomenon has been termed the *commitment effect*. Another way of considering this phenomenon is to state that the "seen mugshot" becomes familiar, and this familiarity increases the likelihood that the person will be identified as the perpetrator in the lineup.

Perfect and Harris (2003) examined the commitment effect in younger (mean age = 22 years) and older (mean age = 71 years) participants who were presented with four photographs and told to study them. The first study consisted of viewing young adult faces. While participants viewed the photographs, the experimenter read four facts about each person in the photographs. Each photograph was displayed to the participants for approximately 10 seconds. After a delay of 30 minutes, participants were then shown mugshots of people who were not one of the four people shown in the photographs. Participants had to decide whether or not they had seen those faces during the first session. One week later, participants were presented with two target-absent lineups that were either all male or all female; furthermore, each lineup contained one face that had been previously shown as a mugshot. Older adults were more likely to exhibit the commitment effect such that they were more likely than the younger adults to choose the previously viewed mugshot out of the lineup. Perfect and Harris followed up this study with two more studies that used older adult faces as stimuli. Results from these two studies did not show the same patterns as when young adult faces were used; the age differences in rates of the commitment effect were removed. However, the researchers speculated that these findings were due to the fact that the young adult's performance decreased when the older faces were used rather than due to an increase in the older adult's performance.

Behrman and Vayder (1994) examined whether a showup had an effect on a subsequent lineup identification task. Participants viewed a videotape of a mock bicycle theft and then were randomly assigned to one of four lineup conditions: control target-present (TP) or target-absent (TA) lineup and experimental TP or TA lineup. Those in the experimental conditions were shown a misleading photograph of an innocent suspect and were told that the man in the photograph had been picked up a short time after the crime had occurred because he fit the general description of the perpetrator. After a 1-week delay, participants viewed the lineup and were asked to make a choice of whether or not the target was present. Those in the experimental condition were significantly more likely to choose the previously seen photograph out of the lineup than those in the control condition, thus providing support for the mugshot commitment effect; approximately 40% of those who had viewed the showup prior to the lineup misidentified the innocent suspect. Furthermore, Behrman and Vayder discussed the prerequisites that were met for the effect to have occurred. Participants had a weak memory trace for the perpetrator, which is shown by the experimental group having a higher proportion of false alarms, specifically choosing the previously seen photograph, than the control group. Second, there was a high degree of physical similarity (Read, Tollestrup, et al., 1990) between the target and the photograph shown in the experimental conditions.

Lamson and Behrman (1997) further examined the effects of viewing a showup prior to a lineup identification task. Participants viewed a video of a mock crime depicting a car theft. They were then randomly assigned to one of three preliminary identification groups: control, showup, or lineup. Participants in the showup condition viewed a showup picture and were told that the suspect had been picked up by the police in the vicinity of the crime. Those in the lineup condition were shown lineup photos and told that a suspect had been picked up by the police. One week later, participants were presented with the lineup task. There were more false identifications of the innocent suspect made by both the preliminary showup and lineup participants than those in the control condition (Lamson & Behrman, 1997). In comparing the preliminary showup and lineup conditions, the showup condition had a higher rate of false identifications. These results suggest that because the showup procedure is biasing, this may increase the likelihood of a commitment effect to occur in the subsequent lineup.

Memon, Hope, Bartlett, and Bull (2002) examined the effect of prior mugshot exposure on lineup identification accuracy between young (aged 18–30 years) and old (aged 60–80 years) participants who were shown a video of a crime reconstruction from the news depicting a car theft. Participants were then assigned to one of three conditions: control, mugshot only exposure, and mugshot plus context. Participants in the mugshot and mugshot plus context groups were given a target-absent mugshot book and were asked if the thief was present among them and told to choose the picture of the thief. A critical foil was included in the mugshot book that also was included in the subsequent lineup. Participants who had chosen the critical foil out of the mugshot book were more likely to choose that same foil compared to those who did not choose someone out of the lineup; those who chose any photograph from mugshot book (not necessarily the critical foil) were more likely to choose that foil instead of correctly rejecting the lineup. The rate at which the critical foil was chosen was relatively equal between the young and old adults. Although the commitment effect was not directly examined, the results from this study support the idea that an innocent, but previously seen, face can be erroneously identified in a subsequent identification task.

Deffenbacher, Bornstein, and Penrod (2006) took a meta-analytic approach to examine the mugshot exposure effect on subsequent lineup identification tasks ($k = 32$). The overall false alarm rate when viewing a mugshot prior to the lineup task was .37 compared to .15 for the control conditions that did not view a mugshot. Another separate set of studies ($k = 19$) examined the transference effect when mugshots were not shown; rather, a bystander was shown in the same context as the target. When a transference condition had been included (both the bystander and target were seen), the overall rate at which transference errors were made was .33 compared to .16 for the control condition in which the bystander was not seen. These findings support the idea that viewing mugshots prior to the lineup identification task decreases accuracy, which increases the probability that the witness will commit a false alarm. These results suggest that prior mugshot exposure may have more of an effect on identification tasks because mugshots are viewed with a greater degree of thoroughness given that one of the persons shown in the mugshots may be the perpetrator. This is in comparison to viewing an innocent bystander in a mock crime and requires the witness to only perceive the bystander well enough to be encoded (Deffenbacher et al., 2006). There is not much effortful processing involved when viewing the innocent bystander.

In addition to research, the commitment effect also is evident in real-world identifications. For example, Earl Patrick Charles was wrongfully convicted based, in part, on faulty eyewitness identification. An armed robbery turned murder occurred in a furniture store in which the eyewitnesses to the crime were employees. Both eyewitnesses were asked to look through mugshots on two different occasions, and although Charles' mugshot was among them, neither eyewitness identified him (The National Registry of Exonerations, 2019). However, Charles was still arrested based on one of the eyewitnesses' claim to have seen the killers in town. When presented with a lineup, the eyewitness identified Charles. The defense attorneys were never informed of the fact that Charles was *not* identified in the previous two mugshot viewings. Charles was charged and convicted of murder and spent 3 years in prison. Seeing Charles downtown may have triggered the eyewitness' memory of seeing him, albeit not fully remembering where he was seen previously. The eyewitness may have misattributed her memory to seeing him in the mugshots, thus leading to a misidentification of an innocent person when presented with the lineup.

A Caveat: When Your Sense of Familiarity Is Wrong

As we have illustrated at various points throughout this book, sometimes a person's sense that they "know that person" or "have seen that person before" is incorrect or misplaced. We have described several ways in which a sense of familiarity may arise and several real-life cases in which this sense of familiarity was incorrect and led to the conviction of an innocent person. It is worth reiterating that an EV's claim of being familiar with the perpetrator may be correct or incorrect. It is essential that police investigate without the assumption that the familiar person is in fact the perpetrator.

Conclusion

Interviewing protocols and lineup procedures are critical for collecting eyewitness evidence. The witnessing of a familiar-stranger commit a crime may interact with both the protocol that is used to interview the witness and the lineup procedure that is used to gain identification evidence. We are just beginning to understand how being familiar with the perpetrator (or believing one is familiar with the perpetrator) influences eyewitness testimony. Further work is needed to understand the interaction between system variables and "familiarity" before any recommendations can be made, although open-ended, nonleading questioning and lineup procedures that emphasize an "absolute" judgment may be particularly useful.

References

Barron, R. M., & Kenny, D. A. (1986). The moderator–mediator variable distinction in social psychological research: Conceptual, strategic, and statistical considerations. *Journal of Personality and Social Psychology, 51*(6), 1173–1182.

Behrman, B., & Vayder, L. (1994). The biasing influence of a police showup: Does the observation of a single suspect taint later identification? *Perceptual and Motor Skills, 79*, 1239–1248.

Bothwell, R., Deffenbacher, K., & Brigham, J. (1987). Correlation of eyewitness accuracy and confidence: Optimality hypothesis revisited. *Journal of Applied Psychology, 72*(4), 691–695. doi:10.1037/0021-9010.72.4.691

Brewer, N., & Wells, G. L. (2006). The confidence–accuracy relationship in eyewitness identification: Effects of lineup instructions, foil similarity, and target-absent base rates. *Journal of Experimental Psychology: Applied, 12*, 11–30. doi:10.1037/1076-898X.12.1.11

Bruce, V., Henderson, Z., Newman, C., & Burton, A. (2001). Matching identities of familiar and unfamiliar faces caught on CCTV images. *Journal of Experimental Psychology: Applied, 7*(3), 207–218.

Bruer, K., & Pozzulo, J. (2014). Familiarity and recall memory for environments: A comparison of children and adults. *Journal of Applied Developmental Psychology, 35*(4), 318–325. doi:10.1016/j.appdev.2014.05.002

Carlson, C. A., Young, D. F., Weatherford, D. R., Carlson, M. A., Bednarz, J. E., & Jones, A. R. (2016). The influence of perpetrator exposure time and weapon presence/timing on eyewitness confidence and accuracy. *Applied Cognitive Psychology, 30*(6), 989–910. doi:10.1002/acp.3275

Cordón, I. M., Silberkleit, G., & Goodman, G. S. (2016). Getting to know you: Familiarity, stereotypes, and children's eyewitness memory. *Behavioral Sciences & the Law, 34*(1), 74–94.

Davis, D., Loftus, E., Vanous, S., & Cucciare, M. (2008). "Unconscious transference" can be an instance of "change blindness." *Applied Cognitive Psychology, 22*, 605–623. doi:10.1002/acp.1395

Deffenbacher, K., Bornstein, B., & Penrod, S. (2006). Mugshot exposure effects: Retroactive interference, mugshot commitment, source confusion, and unconscious transference. *Law and Human Behavior, 30*, 287–307. doi:10.1007/s10979-006-9008-1

Dovidio, J. F., & Gaertner, S. L. (2010). Intergroup bias. In S. T. Fiske, D. T., Gilbert, & G. Lindzey (Eds.), *Handbook of social psychology* (pp. 1084–1121). Hoboken, NJ: Wiley.

Fisher, R. P., & Geiselman, R. E. (1992). *Memory enhancing techniques for investigative interviewing: The cognitive interview.* Springfield, IL: Charles C Thomas.

Gabbert, F., Hope, L., & Fisher, R. (2009). Protecting eyewitness evidence: Examining a self-administered interview tool. *Law and Human Behavior, 33*(4), 298–307.

Geiselman, R. E., Fisher, R. P., Firstenberg, I., Hutton, L. A., Sullivan, S. J., Avetissian, I. V., & Prosk, A. L. (1984). Enhancement of eyewitness memory: An empirical evaluation of the cognitive interview. *Journal of Police Sciences and Administration, 12*, 74–80.

Ginet, M., Py, J., & Colomb, C. (2014). The differential effectiveness of the cognitive interview instructions for enhancing witnesses' memory of a familiar event. *Swiss Journal of Psychology, 73*(1), 25–34.

Humphries, J. E., Holliday, R. E., & Flowe, H. D. (2012). Faces in motion: Age-related changes in eyewitness identification performance in simultaneous, sequential, and elimination video lineups. *Applied Cognitive Psychology, 26*, 149–158. doi:10.1002/acp.1808

Innocence Project. (2019). *Levon Brooks*. Retrieved January 19, 2019, from https://www.innocenceproject.org/cases/levon-brooks

Kleider, H., Pezdek, K., Goldinger, S., & Kirk, A. (2008). Schema-driven source misattribution errors: Remembering the expected from a witnessed event. *Applied Cognitive Psychology, 22*, 1–20. doi:10.1002/acp.1361

Lamson, N., & Behrman, B. (1997). The biasing effect of the photographic showup compared to the lineup on later lineup identification. *Proceedings of the Human Factors and Ergonomics Society Annual Meeting, 41*, 538–542.

Leichtman, M. D., & Ceci, S. J. (1995). The effects of stereotypes and suggestions on preschoolers' reports. *Developmental Psychology, 31*(4), 568–578.

Lepore, S. J., & Sesco, B. (1994). Distorting children's reports and interpretations of events through suggestion. *Journal of Applied Psychology, 79*(1), 108–120. doi:10.1037/0021-9010.79.1.108

L indsay, R. C. L., & Wells, G. L. (1985). Improving eyewitness identification from lineups: Simultaneous and sequential lineup presentation. *Journal of Applied Psychology, 70*, 556–564.

Loftus, E. F. (1976). Unconscious transference in eyewitness identification. *Law and Psychological Review, 2*, 93–98.

Lucas, C. A., & Brewer, N. (2015). Eyewitness identification when "The perpetrator reminds me of someone I know." *Psychiatry, Psychology and Law, 22*(1), 49–59.

Memon, A., Holliday, R., & Hill, C. (2006). Pre-event stereotypes and misinformation effects in young children. *Memory, 14*(1), 104–114.

Memon, A., Hope, L., Bartlett, J., & Bull, R. (2002). Eyewitness recognition errors: The effects of mugshot viewing and choosing in young and old adults. *Memory and Cognition, 30*, 1219–1227.

Migueles, M., & Garcia-Bajos, E. (2012). The power of script knowledge and selective retrieval in the recall of daily activities. *Journal of General Psychology, 139*(2), 100–113. doi:10.1080/00221309.2012.663817

Palmer, M. A., Brewer, N., Weber, N., & Nagesh, A. (2013). The confidence–accuracy relationship for eyewitness identification decisions: Effects of exposure duration, retention interval, and divided attention. *Journal of Experimental Psychology: Applied, 19*, 55–71. doi:10.1037/a0031602

Perfect, T., & Harris, L. (2003). Adult age differences in unconscious transference: Source confusion or identity blending? *Memory and Cognition, 31*, 570–580.

Pozzulo, J. D., Dempsey, J., & Crescini, C. (2009). Preschoolers' person description and identification accuracy: A comparison of the simultaneous and elimination lineup procedures. *Journal of Applied Developmental Psychology, 30*, 667–676. doi:10.1016/j.appdev.2009.01.004

Pozzulo, J. D., Dempsey, J., & Pettalia, J. (2013). The Z generation: Examining perpetrator descriptions and lineup identification procedures. *Journal of Police and Criminal Psychology, 28*, 63–74. doi:10.1007/s11896-012-9107-5

Pozzulo, J. D., & Lindsay, R. C. L. (1998). Identification accuracy of children versus adults: A meta-analysis. *Law and Human Behavior, 22*, 549–570.

Pozzulo, J. D., & Lindsay, R. C. L. (1999). Elimination lineups: An improved identification procedure for child eyewitnesses. *Journal of Applied Psychology, 84*(2), 167–176.

Pozzulo, J. D., Reed, J., Pettalia, J., & Dempsey, J. (2015). Simultaneous, sequential, elimination, and wildcard: A comparison of lineup procedures. *Journal of Police and Criminal Psychology, 31*, 71–80. doi:10.1007/s11896-015-9168-3

Read, J. D., Tollestrup, P., Hammersley, R., McFadzen, E., & Christensen, A. (1990). The unconscious transference effect: Are innocent bystanders ever misidentified? *Applied Cognitive Psychology, 4*, 3–31.

Read, J. D., Vokey, J. R., & Hammersley, R. (1990). Changing photos of faces: Effects of exposure duration and photo similarity on recognition and the accuracy–confidence relationship. *Journal of Experimental Psychology: Learning, Memory, and Cognition, 16*(5), 870–882. doi:10.1037/0278-7393.16.5.870

Ross, D., Ceci, S., Dunning, D., & Toglia, M. (1994). Unconscious transference and mistaken identity: When a witness misidentifies a familiar but innocent person. *Journal of Applied Psychology, 79*, 918–930.

Ross, D., Marsil, D., Benton, T., Hoffman, R., Warren, A., Lindsay, R., & Metzger, R. (2006). Children's susceptibility to misidentifying a familiar bystander from a lineup: When younger is better. *Law and Human Behavior, 30*, 249–257. doi:10.1007/s10979-006-9034-z

Sheahan, C. L., Pica, E., Pozzulo, J., & Nastasa, C. (2017). Eyewitness recall and identification abilities of adolescent and young-adults. *Journal of Applied Developmental Psychology, 53*, 86–95.

Sheahan, C. L., & Pozzulo, J. D. (2019). *"I know that guy!": Familiarity, lineup procedure, and the adolescent witness.* Unpublished manuscript.

Simons, D. J., & Levin, D. T. (1998). Failure to detect changes to people during a real-world interaction. *Psychonomic Bulletin and Review, 5*, 644–649.

Steblay, N., Dysart, J., Fulero, S., & Lindsay, R. C. L. (2001). Eyewitness accuracy rates in sequential and simultaneous lineup presentations: A meta-analytic comparison. *Law and Human Behavior, 25*(5), 459–473.

Steblay, N. K., Dysart, J. E., & Wells, G. L. (2011). Seventy-two tests of the sequential lineup superiority effect: A meta-analysis and policy discussion. *Psychology, Public Policy, and Law, 17*, 99–193. doi:10.1037/a0021650

The National Registry of Exonerations. (2019). *Earl Patrick Charles*. Retrieved January 18, 2019, from https://www.law.umich.edu/special/exoneration/Pages/casedetailpre1989.aspx?caseid=54

Wall, P. (1965). *Eyewitness identification in criminal cases.* Springfield, IL: Charles C Thomas.

Wells, G. L. (1978). Applied eyewitness-testimony research: System variables and estimator variables. *Journal of Personality and Social Psychology, 36*(12), 1546–1557. doi: http://dx.doi.org/10.1037/0022-3514.36.12.1546

Wells, G. (1993). What do we know about eyewitness identification? *American Psychologist, 48*(5), 553–571. doi:10.1037/0003-066X.48.5.553

Wright, A. M., & Holliday, R. E. (2007). Enhancing the recall of young, young-old and old-old adults with cognitive interviews. *Applied Cognitive Psychology, 21*(1), 19–43.

Yuille, J. C., Hunter, R., Joffe, R., & Zaparniuk, J. (1993). Interviewing children in sexual abuse cases. In G. S. Goodman & B. L. Bottoms (Eds.), *Child victims, child witnesses: Understanding and improving testimony* (pp. 95–115). New York, NY: Guilford.

6

Factors That Can Interact with Familiarity

Estimator Variables

As discussed in Chapter 5, an *estimator variable* is a term coined by Wells (1978) to denote those variables that are present at the time of the crime and cannot be changed. Consider the type of lighting that was available as the perpetrator stole the woman's purse while she waited for the bus. Unfortunately, the justice system is "stuck" with the variables that are present at the time of the crime. The degree of familiarity an eyewitness–victim (EV) has with the perpetrator is an estimator variable. Estimator variables do not operate independently, however. Any estimator variable can interact with any other estimator variable(s), as well as system variables (variables that can be manipulated after the crime; Wells, 1978; for more details on system variables, see Chapter 5, this volume). In this chapter, we examine some of the common estimator variables that have been explored in the literature and how they may interact with familiarity.

Role of the Eyewitness: Bystander Versus Victim

Although for much of the book we have used the term eyewitness to include both those who witness a crime and those who also are a victim of a crime, these two roles differ along many dimensions, perhaps the most critical of which is that of the experienced stress, fear, and ultimately level of arousal that a victim may experience compared to an eyewitness. An eyewitness witnessing a crime, who is out of danger, presumably would have a lower level of arousal compared to a victim experiencing harm. Level of arousal or stress

Familiarity and Conviction in the Criminal Justice System. Joanna Pozzulo, Emily Pica, and Chelsea Sheahan, Oxford University Press (2020). © Oxford University Press
DOI: 10.1093/oso/9780190874810.001.0001

can impact the accuracy of an eyewitness (Deffenbacher, Bornstein, Penrod, & McGorty, 2004).

In a meta-analysis by Deffenbacher et al. (2004), arousal was construed as cognitive anxiety and somatic anxiety. *Cognitive anxiety* refers to the worry one feels, whereas *somatic anxiety* refers to one's conscious perception of physiological change (p. 688). The researchers examined the influence of stress on eyewitness identification across 27 independent tests on identification abilities and the influence of stress on recall details across 36 tests. They found that high levels of stress, producing both high cognitive anxiety and high somatic anxiety, can decrease an eyewitness' identification accuracy, although a variety of associations have been found with regard to arousal and eyewitness accuracy (Behrman & Davey, 2001; Morgan et al., 2004; Tollestrup, Turtle, & Yuille, 1994). Under some conditions, arousal/stress has been found to enhance memory. Consider the victim who states, "I was scared to death, I will never forget that face." Under other conditions, arousal/stress has been found to hinder memory. Consider the eyewitness who states, "I was so afraid, I couldn't focus, I don't remember anything." Yet under other conditions, arousal/stress may have no impact. Consider the eyewitness who states, "I was scared for the victim but I wasn't worried for myself. I don't think the stress influenced me."

One explanation for the relationship between stress/arousal and memory is the Yerkes–Dodson law (Yerkes & Dodson, 1908), which proposes that a moderate level of arousal is optimal for best memory performance, whereas too much arousal or too little arousal produces more of an impaired memory. High arousal may cause a person to become overwhelmed, thus leading to a decrease in attention and the ability to encode details for later recall or recognition. An example of this is the situation in which a person who is about to take a driver's test exam does not realize that someone walked off with the purse of a woman who also is waiting. Conversely, when someone has low arousal, he or she may not be paying attention, which again inhibits the ability to later recall information. An example of this is the situation in which someone who recently woke up and went to the corner fast-food restaurant for breakfast does not realize that the cashier is being held up. The Yerkes–Dodson law is shown in Figure 6.1 as an inverted U function, where moderate levels of arousal result in the best memory performance.

"Optimal arousal" may vary depending on the context and the person as well as the degree of familiarity to the perpetrator. Due to individual differences (which are discussed more in-depth later), the optimal level of arousal varies among people. We may speculate that seeing a familiar perpetrator may decrease arousal. However, a familiar perpetrator engaged in criminal activity where you are the victim at the hands of this familiar person may raise arousal. On the other hand, a bystander who witnesses a familiar perpetrator may feel less arousal, believing that the risk for harm is lower than that if witnessing an unfamiliar perpetrator. Whether a familiar perpetrator raises arousal higher than the level of arousal for a perpetrator who is a

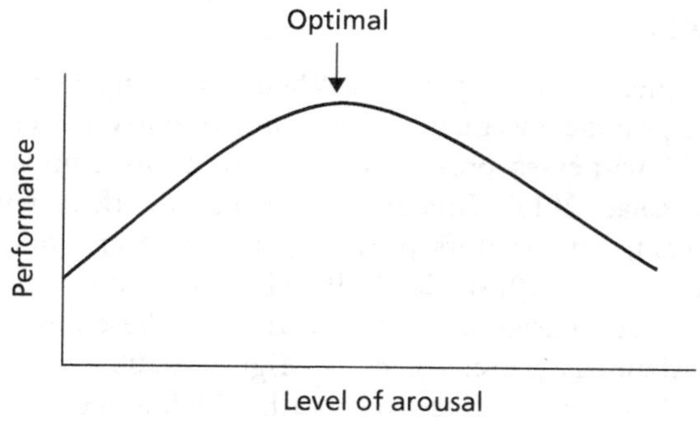

Figure 6.1 Yerkes–Dodson law.
Source: Reproduced from Cohen, R. A. (2011). Yerkes-Dodson Law. In J. S. Kreutzer, J. DeLuca., & B. Caplan (Eds.), *Encyclopedia of clinical neuropsychology*. New York, NY: Springer.

complete stranger is unclear, as is how familiarity interacts with the role of the eyewitness, as either bystander or victim. Further research should consider arousal and a sense of familiarity with the perpetrator.

Weapon Presence

Related to the amount of arousal that witnessing or experiencing a crime can induce is whether a weapon is present during a crime. A perpetrator holding a weapon can significantly increase arousal compared to if a weapon is present, in that a weapon may prove deadly. The weapon may garner more attention than the perpetrator given the potential for violence that a weapon may inflict.

Easterbrook (1959) proposed the cue-utilization hypothesis to help explain why a witness may focus on one detail more so than another. The cue-utilization hypothesis postulates that as emotional arousal increases, attentional capacity decreases. When attentional capacity is limited, central details such as a weapon are more likely to be encoded compared to more peripheral details such as hair color. Thus, high levels of arousal will more than likely be detrimental to the recall of a perpetrator and/or the crime itself regardless of whether the eyewitness and perpetrator are familiar with each other. Speculating, a familiar perpetrator holding a weapon may lead the witness to focus on the weapon; when having to recall and identify the perpetrator, the witness may rely on stereotypes (i.e., the projection of an individual's own expectations and beliefs onto another individual despite insufficient factual knowledge about the respective individual; Fiske, 2010; see also Chapter 2, this volume) to a greater extent than if the perpetrator was a stranger to fill in memory gaps. The role of a weapon should be examined when trying to delineate an eyewitness' accuracy with a familiar perpetrator.

Age of Witness

Victims and witnesses can be any age. When describing a stranger, younger child witnesses provide fewer descriptors compared to older child witnesses, and older child witnesses provide fewer descriptors compared to adults (Jack, Leov, & Zajac, 2014). This pattern seems to shift as witnesses reach their senior years, with seniors providing fewer descriptors compared to adults (Pica & Pozzulo, 2018). Generally, although older witnesses provide more descriptors compared to younger witnesses, these descriptors are not less accurate (Aizpurua, Garcia-Bajos, & Migueles, 2009; List, 1986; Yarmey & Kent, 1980). Moreover, the accuracy with which a descriptor is reported is also influenced by the nature of the descriptor (Sheahan, Pica, Pozzulo, & Nastasa, 2017). For example, describing a stranger's age becomes challenging if the age of the stranger is outside the witness' cohort (i.e., approximately a 10-year age span from the witness' age; Pozzulo & Warren, 2003). Eye color, on the other hand, seems to be difficult for witnesses of any age (Kuehn, 1974; van Koppen & Lochun, 1997).

Identifying strangers also appears problematic for younger witnesses compared to older witnesses (Fitzgerald & Price, 2015; Pozzulo & Lindsay, 1998). Children have greater difficulty with correct identification and correct rejection compared to adults (Pozzulo & Lindsay, 1998). In addition, seniors have greater difficulty with correct identification and correct rejection compared to younger adults (Fitzgerald & Price, 2015). Identification procedures (as discussed in Chapter 5, this volume) can influence a witness' accuracy, with different procedures being more effective for some age ranges compared to others.

No studies to date have examined the effect of familiarity of the perpetrator and age of the witness on the ability to describe and/or identify a perpetrator. It may be that the developmental pattern demonstrated for stranger descriptions and identification is less prominent or may disappear with a "familiar" description and identification provided by younger and older eyewitnesses. As familiarity increases, children's level of inaccuracy may decrease to a point at which there is no difference in identification accuracy between children and adults. Even very young children rarely mistake their mother or father.

Considering the notion of identification of someone familiar, Pozzulo, Dempsey, Bruer, and Sheahan (2012) examined young children (aged 4–7 years) and adults who were shown a series of targets that were either familiar (i.e., popular cartoon characters) or unfamiliar (human faces). It was predicted that any differences in identification accuracy between children and adults would disappear for the familiar cartoon characters. Children produced essentially a 100% correct identification rate for the cartoon characters; however, they produced a significantly lower correct rejection rate for these characters compared to adults. Familiarity can improve children's (and adult's) correct identification rates, but the tendency to make an identification may be very strong for some, such that even with very familiar targets, that false positive identifications may occur with target-absent lineups, particularly for child witnesses. However, there may be fewer errors with the identification of familiar-strangers than complete strangers.

Examining the real-life case of Elizabeth Smart (as detailed in Chapter 1, this volume), Elizabeth's sister, Mary Margaret, identified Elizabeth's abductor as someone "familiar." Mary Margaret was correct. Of course, this is anecdotal and certainly we could find a case in which a youngster erred in thinking the perpetrator was familiar when in fact he or she was not, such as the case of Clarence Elkins, who was identified as the perpetrator by his niece (detailed in Chapter 1, this volume). A more fulsome discussion of a witness' perception of familiarity when the perpetrator may not in fact be familiar is provided in Chapter 7.

Race

First, a note on the term "race." Race is a broad umbrella term that has been used in the eyewitness literature for many years. Given that we are reviewing that literature, we use the term but acknowledge that it is imprecise and it can be difficult to categorize individuals this way; however, as mentioned previously, for consistency with the literature, we use the term.

A substantial amount of research has been conducted examining the influence of "race" on potential eyewitness accuracy. The cross-race effect is defined as the ability to describe and identify those of one's own race more accurately than those of other races (Meissner & Brigham, 2001). For example, a White eyewitness may be better able to correctly identify another White person than a Black person and vice versa (Young, Hugenberg, Bernstein, & Sacco, 2012). An Asian may be better able to correctly identify another Asian than a White or Black person and vice versa (Hayward, Rhodes, & Schwaninger, 2008).

A number of hypotheses have been put forth to understand the cross-race effect.

Attitudes

It has been suggested that people who have less prejudicial attitudes are more accurate at recognizing those from other races (Walker & Hewstone, 2008). However, the research thus far does not seem to provide support for this explanation (Meissner & Brigham, 2001; Slone, Brigham, & Meissner, 2000). Although Meissner and Brigham suggested that prejudicial attitudes may be associated with the amount of contact (discussed later) a person has with other-race members, that in turn may influence how accurate one is in identifying those from other races.

Physiognomic Homogeneity

Some have suggested that the other-race effect may be a result of some races' faces having less variability in their appearance. The notion here is one of "They all look alike." This explanation has not received much empirical support, however. For example, in a study by Goldstein (1979), Japanese, Black, and White faces were examined, and members of each group were not deemed any more similar than members belonging to a different group. However, similarity may not be the issue—that is, the descriptors people use to describe a face may be more appropriate for one group than another. For example, there may be more variability in hair color for White faces compared to Black faces. However, hair color dyes can be found fairly easily throughout the world, making hair color easily changeable for many, regardless of race. In contrast, facial structures may have more similarity among one race compared to other races (Sporer, 2001); however, describing these features may be more difficult than naming hair colors. Overall, physiognomic homogeneity does not appear to sufficiently explain the cross-race effect.

Interracial Contact

Perhaps the explanation for the cross-race effect receiving the most empirical attention is the amount of contact individuals have with other races. Essentially, the more contact one has with other races, the more accurate one will be at identifying those from other races. In one test of this hypothesis, Li, Dunning, and Malpass (1998, as cited in Meissner & Brigham, 2001) examined the ability of White basketball "experts" (i.e., dedicated fans) and White basketball novices to recognize Black faces. Given that the majority of professional basketball players in the United States are Black, it was predicted that the experts would have more experience distinguishing Black faces and hence be more accurate at identifying Black faces compared to the novices. Support for this prediction was found. However, not all studies that have investigated interracial contact have found the predicted effect. For example, Ng and Lindsay (1994) examined university students from Canada and Singapore, and the other-race effect was not completely supported. A definitive conclusion on the contact hypothesis and how it factors into the other-race effect remains unclear. Having voluntary, "quality" contact may be helpful at remediating the cross-race effect, but it may not be the complete explanation for why the effect occurs.

To date, the association between familiarity and race has not been examined. It would be an interesting avenue for research given that many cases have a cross-race component. For example, the Innocence Project has found that in cases involving eyewitness identification, more than half included cross-race individuals (Innocence Project, 2017). It is speculated that as familiarity increases, so does identification accuracy of an individual belonging to another race. It would be interesting to determine whether those who live in predominately other-race communities are more accurate in identifying those belonging to other races.

Consider the case of Michael Phillips discussed in Chapter 1. In addition to the feeling of familiarity, the cross-race effect also may have played a role in his conviction. Phillips was an African American, whereas the victim was Caucasian. The victim was attacked in her motel room and identified the attacker as Phillips, whom she had seen living at the motel. She identified him from a six-person photographic lineup; he later pled guilty to avoid the possibility of receiving a sentence of life in prison (The National Registry of Exonerations, 2019a). Although DNA was available, it was not tested at the time of the crime. Nineteen years later, the DNA from the crime scene was tested, and Phillips was determined to be innocent of the crime in question. Yet another example is the case of Walter Snyder, an African American, also involving a cross-racial identification by a Caucasian victim. The victim was attacked in her home after the perpetrator broke in her door (Innocence Project, 2019). The police presented the victim with a showup containing a picture of Snyder, whom she identified as living across the street from her. Snyder spent 7 years in prison because laboratory work examining the blood found at the crime scene did not exclude Snyder as the perpetrator. After 7 years, the blood evidence was retested, and this time the DNA report excluded Snyder as a match (The National Registry of Exonerations, 2019b). There are numerous cases that involve cross-race issues with a sense of familiarity between the EV and alleged perpetrator. Well-designed empirical studies would be useful for understanding how familiarity and race interact to influence perpetrator descriptions and identifications.

Personality Variables

A number of personality traits may interact with eyewitness memory and familiarity of the perpetrator (Pozzulo, Coplan, & Wilson, 2005). Because of the challenges in understanding and assessing personality, its applicability to the criminal justice system may be limited. Police officers, for example, may not have the training or desire to administer personality tests to witnesses. Nonetheless, understanding how personality may interact or influence a witness' memory report can be important when evaluating eyewitness evidence. Moreover, one cluster of personality traits that have been examined with applicability to the witnessing condition is how one feels when around other people, specifically introverted or extroverted—somewhat relatedly being shy or not shy.

Extroversion and neuroticism, as part of Eysenck's personality test (Eysenck, 1947; Eysenck & Eysenck, 1964), have been examined in the context of "eyewitnessing." According to Eysenck and colleagues, four personality traits are essential in understanding an individual: extraversion–introversion and emotionality–stability. An individual will fall somewhere between each of the two poles, indicating his or her personality characteristics. Unfortunately, Areh and Umek (2007) found that it was not possible to predict a witness' ability to be a good eyewitness.

Pozzulo and colleagues (2005) examined whether shy versus non-shy witnesses would produce more accurate memory reports and identification rates. It was hypothesized that shyness would facilitate witness accuracy under some conditions. In Experiment 1, witnesses were asked to respond to directed recall questions probing a crime event and perpetrator details. Non-shy and shy witnesses produced comparable accuracy rates when describing the perpetrator. In contrast, non-shy witnesses were more accurate when describing crime environment details compared to shy witnesses. In Experiment 2, arousal was manipulated, and a free recall approach was used to assess recall accuracy. Under low arousal, shy witnesses were more accurate at describing the perpetrator compared to non-shy witnesses, whereas non-shy witnesses were more accurate at describing crime details compared to shy witnesses. Under high arousal, differences in accuracy were not observed across shy and non-shy witnesses. It is likely that personality interacts with a number of other factors and may have differential effects depending on whether one is describing the perpetrator, environment, or making an identification.

To date, individual differences have not been examined in the context of familiarity with the perpetrator. However, we speculate that some familiarity with the perpetrator may interact with individual differences to influence recall and identification. For example, for a shy eyewitness, being somewhat familiar with the perpetrator and/or crime scene may be helped by this familiarity in that the familiarity decreases arousal and may improve accuracy when describing and identifying the perpetrator more so than for a non-shy witness who does not require a degree of familiarity to reduce arousal in order to facilitate recall and identification.

Conclusion

This chapter highlights a number of variables that can co-occur with familiarity and can interact to ultimately influence a witness' recall and identification. Estimator variables interact with each other as well as with system variables (see Chapter 5) such as interview protocols and lineup procedures. It is clear that when trying to evaluate eyewitness evidence, a myriad of factors coalesce to influence accuracy. The challenge for the criminal justice system is to weigh the various factors and give some value to the eyewitness testimony. As researchers, we tend to focus on main effects and individual variables, which is a good starting point; however, if we are to provide any useful information to the criminal justice system, we also must start to evaluate combinations of factors and their ultimate influence on eyewitness recall and identification accuracy. When considering real-life crime, a majority of crime involves familiarity, yet little research has considered how familiarity interacts with other estimator (and/or system) variables. Moving forward, it is essential that we vary familiarity along with other factors.

References

Aizpurua, A., Garcia-Bajos, E., & Migueles, M. (2009). Memory for actions of an event: Older and younger adults compared. *Journal of General Psychology, 136*, 1–14.

Areh, I., & Umek, P. (2007). Predicting quality of memory recall by personality traits. *Studia Psychologica, 49*(1), 19–26.

Behrman, B. W., & Davey, S. L. (2001). Eyewitness identification in actual criminal cases: An archival analysis. *Law and Human Behavior, 25*, 475–491. doi:10.1023/A:1012840831846

Deffenbacher, K., Bornstein, B., Penrod, D., & McGorty, K. (2004). A meta-analytic review of the effects of high stress on eyewitness memory. *Law and Human Behavior, 28*(6), 687–706. doi:10.1007/s10979-004-0565-x

Easterbrook, J. A. (1959). The effect of emotion on cue utilization and the organization of behavior. *Psychological Review, 66*(3), 183–201. doi:10.1037/h0047707

Eysenck, H. J. (1947). Screening out the neurotic. *Lancet, 249*, 530–521.

Eysenck, S. B. G., & Eysenck, H. J. (1964). An improved short questionnaire for the measurement of extraversion and neuroticism. *Life Sciences, 3*(10), 1103–1109. doi:10.1016/0024-3205(64)90125-0

Fiske, S. T. (2010). Venus and Mars or down to Earth: Stereotypes and realities of gender differences. *Perspectives on Psychological Science, 5*(6), 688–692. doi:10.1177/1745691610388768

Fitzgerald, R., & Price, H. (2015). Eyewitness identification across the life span: A meta-analysis of age differences. *Psychological Bulletin, 141*, 1228–1265. doi:10.1037/bul0000013

Goldstein, A. G. (1979). Race-related variation of facial features: Anthropometric data I. *Bulletin of the Psychonomic Society, 13*, 187–190.

Hayward, W., Rhodes, G., & Schwaninger, A. (2008). An own-race advantage for components as well as configurations in face recognition. *Cognition, 106*(2), 1017–1027. doi:10.1016/j.cognition.2007.04.002

Innocence Project. (2017). *DNA exonerations in the United States.* Retrieved October 6, 2017, from https://www.innocenceproject.org/dna-exonerations-in-the-united-states

Innocence Project. (2019). *Walter Snyder.* Retrieved January 19, 2019, from https://www.innocenceproject.org/cases/walter-snyder

Jack, F., Leov, J., & Zajac, R. (2014). Age-related differences in the free-recall accounts of child, adolescent, and adult witnesses. *Applied Cognitive Psychology, 28*, 30–38. doi:10.1002/acp.2951

Kuehn, L. L. (1974). Looking down a gun barrel: Person perception and violent crime. *Perceptual and Motor Skills, 39*, 1159–1164.

Li, J. C., Dunning, D., & Malpass, R. S. (1998, March). *Cross-racial identification among European-Americans: Basketball fandom and the contact hypothesis.*

Paper presented at the biennial meeting of the American Psychology-Law Society, Redondo Beach, CA.
List, J. (1986). Age and schematic differences in the reliability of eyewitness testimony. *Developmental Psychology, 22*, 50–57.
Meissner, C., & Brigham, J. (2001). Thirty years of investigating the own-race bias in memory for faces: A meta-analytic review. *Psychology, Public Policy, and Law, 7*(1), 3–35. doi:10.1037/1076-8971.7.1.3
Morgan, C. A., Hazlett, G., Doran, A., Garrett, S., Hoyt, G., Thomas, P., . . . Southwick, S. M. (2004). Accuracy of eyewitness memory for persons encountered during exposure to highly intense stress. *International Journal of Law & Psychiatry, 27*, 265–279. doi:10.1016/j.ijlp.2004.03.004
Ng, W., & Lindsay, R. C. L. (1994). Cross-race facial recognition: Failure of the contact hypothesis. *Journal of Cross-Cultural Psychology, 25*, 217–232.
Pica, E., & Pozzulo, J. (2018). Younger and older adult eyewitness identification: A comparison of the simultaneous, elimination, and wildcard procedures. *Psychiatry, Psychology and Law, 25*, 106–123. doi:10.1080/13218719.2017.1364614
Pozzulo, J. D., Coplan, R. J., & Wilson, J. (2005). Not too "shy" to help catch a thief: Recall memory of shy versus non-shy witnesses. *Personality and Individual Differences, 39*(8), 1361–1372.
Pozzulo, J. D., Dempsey, J., Bruer, K., & Sheahan, C. (2012). The culprit in target-absent lineups: Understanding young children's false positive responding. *Journal of Police and Criminal Psychology, 27*(1), 55–62.
Pozzulo, J. D., & Lindsay, R. C. L. (1998). Identification accuracy of children versus adults: A meta-analysis. *Law and Human Behavior, 22*, 549–570.
Pozzulo, J. D., & Warren, K. L. (2003). Descriptions and identifications of strangers by youth and adult eyewitnesses. *Journal of Applied Psychology, 88*, 315–323. doi:10.1037/002-9010.88.2.315
Sheahan, C., Pica, E., Pozzulo, J., & Nastasa, C. (2017). Eyewitness recall and identification abilities of adolescents and young adults. *Journal of Applied Developmental Psychology, 53*, 86–95. doi:10.1016/j.appdev.2017.09.008
Slone, A., Brigham, J., & Meissner, C. (2000). Social and cognitive factors affecting the own-race bias in Whites. *Basic and Applied Social Psychology, 22*(2), 71–84.
Sporer, S. L. (2001). The cross-race effect: Beyond recognition of faces in the laboratory. *Psychology, Public Policy, and Law, 7*(1), 170–200. doi:10.1037/1076-8971.7.1.170
The National Registry of Exonerations. (2019a). *Michael Phillips*. Retrieved January 18, 2019, from https://www.law.umich.edu/special/exoneration/Pages/casedetail.aspx?caseid=4483
The National Registry of Exonerations. (2019b). *Walter Snyder*. Retrieved January 18, 2019, from https://www.law.umich.edu/special/exoneration/Pages/casedetail.aspx?caseid=3651
Tollestrup, P. A., Turtle, J. W., & Yuille, J. C. (1994). Actual victims and witnesses to robbery and fraud: An archival analysis. In D. F. Ross, J. D., Read, & M. P. Toglia (Eds.), *Adult eyewitness testimony: Current trends and developments* (pp. 144–162). Cambridge, UK: Cambridge University Press.

van Koppen, P. J., & Lochun, S. K. (1997). Portraying perpetrators: The validity of offender descriptions by witnesses. *Law and Human Behavior, 21*(6), 661–685. doi:10.1023/A:1024812831576

Walker, P. M., & Hewstone, M. (2008). The influence of social factors and implicit racial bias on a generalized own-race effect. *Applied Cognitive Psychology, 22*(4), 441–453. doi:10.1002/acp.1382

Wells, G. L. (1978). Applied eyewitness-testimony research. System variables and estimator variables. *Journal of Personality and Social Psychology, 36*, 1546–1557. doi: http://dx.doi.org/10.1037/0022-3514.36.12.1546

Yarmey, A. D., & Kent, J. (1980). Eyewitness identification by elderly and young adults. *Law and Human Behavior, 4*, 359–371.

Yerkes, R. M., & Dodson, J. D. (1908). The relation of strength of stimulus and rapidity of habit formation. *Journal of Comparative Neurology, 18*(5), 459–482. doi:10.1002/cne.920180503

Young, S., Hugenberg, K., Bernstein, M., & Sacco, D. (2012). Perception and motivation in face recognition: A critical review of theories of the cross-race effect. *Personality and Social Psychology Review, 16*(2), 116–142. doi:10.1177/1088868311418987

7

Considering Familiarity as a Dependent Variable

Seeing two or more people at the same time can result in memory errors, such that an innocent bystander during the commission of a crime may be remembered as the perpetrator. The eyewitness cannot accurately remember where the person was seen and confuses the bystander as the perpetrator. The notion of source monitoring is related to this misremembering because the source of the memory is inaccurately recalled. Consider, one Saturday afternoon you see a female waiting for a bus. A male quickly approaches and grabs the woman's bag. Several weeks later, when police show you a lineup, you misidentify a male as the perpetrator. As it turns out, you had seen this male walk his dog in your neighborhood. Your memory for where you recognized the male is incorrect. Occasionally, someone induces a sense of familiarity and one incorrectly attributes a role and/or context to the person to explain the sense of familiarity. Not only may this be a source monitoring issue but also it may be a result of poor witnessing conditions (one is far away from the person, low lighting conditions, etc.) or simply a memory error. Thus, witnessing a crime and then thinking one "knows" the perpetrator may or may not be accurate. This chapter explores these issues and their influence on identification accuracy rates.

Making Familiarity Errors

As described previously, a crime may occur and an innocent bystander is identified in a lineup as the person who committed the crime. As a witness, you may misremember the innocent bystander as being the perpetrator.

Familiarity and Conviction in the Criminal Justice System. Joanna Pozzulo, Emily Pica, and Chelsea Sheahan, Oxford University Press (2020). © Oxford University Press
DOI: 10.1093/oso/9780190874810.001.0001

Possibly because the person you see induces a sense of familiarity, you identify him or her as the perpetrator. This type of error is known as a *source misattribution error.* Thus, a sense of familiarity may lead to an erroneous identification. For example, if an eyewitness is shown a mugshot of the suspect prior to viewing the lineup, the eyewitness may choose this suspect out of the lineup because he or she senses a level of familiarity with that picture. In addition, if there is an innocent bystander at the crime and he or she is also placed in the lineup without the actual perpetrator, the bystander may be chosen because a sense of familiarity is induced given that he or she was seen at the crime scene.

Mugshot Commitment Effects

Commitment or familiarity effects have been studied in a number of ways. In some studies, participants are shown a series of "mugshots" (i.e., in real life, mugshots are photos of previously charged individuals) and told to sort through them to determine if the perpetrator is among the pool of mugshots. A previously seen photo from the mugshot search is then used in a lineup, and the witness is asked to identify the perpetrator if he or she is present. Witnesses are more likely to re-identify the photo initially seen in the mugshot search from the photo array (Brigham & Cairns, 1988). This is known as a *commitment effect*. The witness selected someone from the mugshot search and is now re-seeing him or her in the lineup and re-selects this "familiar" person as the perpetrator.

To illustrate, Brigham and Cairns (1988) examined the effect of prior viewing of mugshots on the ability to make a subsequent lineup identification. Some of the participants rated mugshot photos on the attractiveness of the face or judged whether the perpetrator's photo was present in a group of photographs or presented individually. Two days later, the participants were shown a target-present lineup. For participants in the mugshot condition who selected a mugshot, the photograph they chose was also included in the target-present lineup. Participants who had chosen a mugshot photograph were more likely to incorrectly identify a lineup member other than the perpetrator, usually the person they had previously chosen from the mugshots.

A number of studies have demonstrated this commitment effect (and hence errors in identification) using mugshots to elicit familiarity. For example, Dysart, Lindsay, Hammond, and Dupuis (2001) examined the influence of viewing mugshots on subsequent identification performance. They found that committing to a face when examining mugshots increased misidentifications. In addition, Memon, Hope, Bartlett, and Bull (2002) examined the effect of prior mugshot exposure on lineup identification but included an older adult sample (aged 60–80 years). Participants in the mugshot and mugshot plus context groups (i.e., witnesses were provided with context reinstatement instructions in addition to viewing the mugshots) were then given a target-absent mugshot book and were asked if the thief was present among the mugshots and, if so, told to identify the thief. A critical foil was included in the mugshot book that also was included in the subsequent lineup—that is, one foil photograph appeared in both the mugshots and the lineup task. Participants then proceeded to the lineup task and viewed a target-absent lineup. Participants who had chosen the critical foil out of the mugshot book were more likely to choose that same foil compared to those who did not choose someone out of the lineup; in addition, those who chose any photograph from the mugshot book (not necessarily the critical foil) were more likely to choose that foil instead of correctly rejecting the lineup. The rate at which the critical foil was chosen was relatively equal between the younger and older adults.

Moreover, Lamson and Behrman (1997) examined the effects of viewing a showup (i.e., a single photo of the suspect) prior to a lineup identification task. Participants were placed in one of three conditions: viewing a showup prior to the lineup task, a preliminary lineup prior to the lineup task, and the control condition with no preliminary identification task. Participants in the showup condition viewed a showup and were told that the suspect had been picked up by the police in the vicinity of the crime. More false identifications of the innocent suspect were made by both the preliminary showup and the lineup participants compared to those in the control condition (Lamson & Behrman, 1997). When comparing the preliminary showup and lineup conditions, the showup condition had a higher rate of false identifications. Results suggest that because the showup condition is a biasing procedure (i.e., it may put pressure on the witness to make an identification because he or she knows who the police suspect committed the crime), this may increase the likelihood of a commitment effect when shown a subsequent lineup.

Overall, these studies demonstrate that viewing multiple photos of potential suspects prior to having to make an identification of the perpetrator may influence one's sense of familiarity with an innocent individual. Committing to a face in an initial task increases the likelihood that one will select this face as the target/perpetrator. This familiarity can lead to misidentification whereby an innocent individual is wrongfully identified.

Mere Prior Exposure Effects

Related to commitment effects, it has been demonstrated that the mere exposure to someone is sufficient for the witness to have a sense of familiarity and lead the witness to identify the familiar person as the perpetrator (Memon, Hope, & Bull, 2003). Some studies have found that simply examining mugshots is sufficient to induce familiarity and misidentify a prior seen mugshot, irrespective of whether anyone was chosen from the mugshots (Dysart et al., 2001). Thus, although the person was not seen committing the crime and merely seen in a different context (in this case, in the mugshot search), this is sufficient for later misidentification. Examining a series of mugshots and then seeing one of the faces from the mugshots in a lineup can make witnesses more likely to identify that previously seen mugshot as the perpetrator when in fact he or she is not the perpetrator.

Kersten, Earles, and Upshaw (2013) examined whether people could become associated with actions they performed or participated in. Participants were presented with different events that each involved two people playing two different roles (i.e., one person putting a jacket on another person). Younger adults (mean age = 19.39 years) and older adults (mean age = 71.44 years) in Study 1 were presented with video clips of two confederates taking part in the joint activity. Participants were initially presented with the target event and then presented with either a same-event conjunction (i.e., the person who had the coat put on her was now putting a coat on someone new) or a different-event conjunction (i.e., the person who put a coat on the other person was now performing a different action that was previously seen performed by a different confederate). Overall, participants were more likely to falsely recognize an actor who was performing an action that was previously seen performed by someone else. Older adults were more likely to falsely recognize a novel conjunction of a familiar actor and action regardless of whether they were from the same event or different events. Study 2 employed similar procedures with younger adults (mean age = 20.22 years) and replicated the primary finding of Study 1, whereby participants were more likely to falsely recognize an actor who was performing an action that was previously performed by somebody else if the two actors appeared in the same event (Kersten et al., 2013).

In a related study, Kersten and Earles (2017) examined participants who were younger (mean age = 19.33 years) or older adults (mean age = 71.76 years) viewing actors performing different actions. Participants were asked questions about which actor performed which action, and mugshots of potential targets for the action were presented; half of the participants were then immediately given the event recognition portion, and the other half returned 3 weeks later for the recognition portion. In the recognition portion, participants were again presented with actors performing different actions. Participants were instructed that an actor may be seen performing an action performed by a different actor in the learning (prior) phase. In addition, participants were instructed that they may see an actor performing an action not previously performed but described in relation to the mugshot picture shown. Participants were asked, "Did you see this person perform this action in the first part of the experiment?" If either of the aforementioned instances occurred, participants were instructed to respond "No." Older adults were more likely to falsely recognize a new conjunction of a familiar actor and familiar action if they had seen the mugshot of the actor prior to the recognition phase, regardless of whether the mugshot was accompanied by a question concerning the action. Conversely, young adults were more likely to make an error only if the mugshot had been accompanied by a question about that particular action.

As the previous studies illustrate, the simple act of having seen someone previously is sufficient to lead to recognition errors. Roles can get reversed. Moreover, actions can be misascribed to the wrong individual.

Presence of a Bystander

Seeing someone other than the perpetrator at the time of the crime also can produce a familiarity effect, with this other person being mistaken as the perpetrator when shown in a lineup. For example, Ross et al. (2006) studied children aged 5–12 years ($N = 779$). Participants watched a videotape in which money was stolen from a teacher's bag. Some children were shown a video that included a bystander along with the thief. Following the video, children were shown a lineup. In the bystander condition, the lineup contained the bystander but not the thief. The older children (11- and 12-year-olds) in the bystander condition were more likely to misidentify the familiar bystander as the thief compared to the children in the control condition (i.e., no bystander shown in the video). Being younger seemed to be advantageous because the increase in bystander identifications was not found for the 5- to 10-year-olds. This study demonstrates that the familiarity effect may not necessarily operate the same way across different-aged witnesses.

Overall, eyewitnesses may incorrectly associate the actions of one person with those of another when the two people appear together. Extrapolating to the eyewitness paradigm, if an eyewitness *witnesses* a crime during which multiple people are present, he or she may incorrectly attribute the actions to an innocent bystander when presented with a lineup. This phenomenon can occur with children and adults.

Why Do These Errors Occur?

Research suggests that a sense of familiarity can contribute to erroneous identification under a variety of scenarios. It is important to consider why this phenomenon occurs and possibly determine if and how it can be prevented. Three primary explanations are source monitoring, unconscious transference, and stereotyping.

Source Monitoring

Johnson and Raye (1981) proposed the reality-monitoring frame, which refers to the discriminating of memories that are generated internally from memories of externally derived information. Researchers suggest that source monitoring is an extension of the reality-monitoring frame (Johnson, Hashtroudi, & Lindsay, 1993). Source monitoring can be thought of as the cognitive processes people engage in while identifying the sources of their recollection, and it relies on the quality of information people encode about different events. In essence, the quality of people's memories depends on how the memories are formed. Early research examining source monitoring focused on the recognition of words from a given list. Specifically, Anderson and Bower (1972, 1974) proposed the notion that when people are asked to determine whether words have been previously seen, they cannot solely rely on familiarity due to the fact that all of the words are familiar in some way, shape, or form. Therefore, participants in these types of studies must rely on source monitoring to remember where they specifically remember seeing the word (i.e., the initial source) to determine whether it was seen during the learning phase of the recognition test.

The identification of an innocent individual may be due, in part, to source monitoring errors. Consider the case of Joseph Abbitt discussed in Chapter 1. The witnesses knew that they had seen Abbitt before, but they erroneously recalled the source from where this memory came from. Instead of correctly recalling that Abbitt was a prior neighbor, they believed he was the perpetrator who assaulted them (The National Registry of Exonerations, 2017). Researchers have found that source monitoring errors are especially prevalent when the eyewitness is questioned in a leading or suggestive way. For example, Mitchell, Johnson, and Mather (2003) compared younger and older adults' source monitoring performance in a misinformation paradigm. Participants viewed a 5-minute segment of a police training video that depicted a burglary. After the video, participants were given misleading post-event questions that included incorrect information. Participants were presented with a source memory test to state where they heard the information (i.e., the source). Overall, older adults were more suggestible, and more likely to make source monitoring errors, than were younger adults. Specifically, older adults were more likely to recall having already obtained the information (i.e., old) when in fact the information was presented to them in the post-event questionnaire, thus suggesting that source monitoring errors may increase with age.

Unconscious Transference

Misidentifying a bystander as the perpetrator may be a result of "unconscious transference." Unconsciously, a person transfers the criminal activity to someone nearby. Loftus (1976) was one of the first to examine the unconscious transference effect and developed a paradigm in which participants take part in an experiment during which mugshots are not shown prior to the lineup; instead, they include a bystander who shares context with the target. Specifically, participants were presented with a story via tape recorder with the accompaniment of a picture of each character displayed for 2 seconds when they were introduced. Participants heard the same story but saw different sets of photographs. Half of the participants saw photographs with the criminal among them, and the other half saw the bystander as well. Three days later, the participants were asked to look at a lineup and decide whether the perpetrator was present. More than half of those who saw the bystander's photo were more likely to choose the bystander. The results of this study support the notion that a brief exposure to a person can cause him or her to look familiar when seen later, in a lineup for example. The familiar face is integrated into the participant's memory of the crime, which later increases the likelihood that the bystander will be chosen from the lineup.

A set of follow-up studies provide a better understanding of the conditions under which the bystander effect does or does not occur. For example, Read, Tollestrup, Hammersley, McFadzen, and Christensen (1990) found that an innocent bystander was not more likely to be identified in a lineup task. However, an increase in errors occurred when the perpetrator and bystander looked similar to each other. Including a "familiar," *similar* face in the lineup influenced identification decisions. Thus, similarity appears to enhance familiarity. In addition, Ross, Ceci, Dunning, and Toglia (1994) considered when a witness would be more likely to misidentify a familiar but innocent person. Support was found for unconscious transference, with the bystander significantly more likely to be chosen in the target-absent lineup for participants in the transference condition compared to those in the control condition, in which participants did not see the innocent bystander in the crime video. In the target-present lineup, the transference and control conditions did not differ in their ability to make a correct identification. Thus, if the target is not present in a lineup, witnesses may identify the most familiar person from the options available. If the bystander is present, he or she may be misidentified if the perpetrator is absent.

Ainsworth (1998) used a different approach in studying the effects of unconscious transference. He examined the role of unconscious transference in media crime reporting. Participants read an article about a string of attacks on local females. The article contained a picture of the suspect as well as a picture of a man who had saved one of the female victims. Participants who viewed the bystander-present lineup were more likely to choose the bystander out of the lineup. Although this is not the typical paradigm in which unconscious transference is studied, this study does lend support to unconscious transference. Participants remembered seeing a particular face but did not remember why or where they had seen the face (i.e., a source monitoring error).

Stereotyping

When a person is witness to a crime, he or she may use stereotype-consistent, but inaccurate, details about the crime to fill in the gaps of his or her memory. For example, as discussed in Chapter 6, the cross-race identification can impact identification rates whereby identifying someone from another race decreases accuracy (Meissner & Brigham, 2001). Also, just looking prototypically Black may induce wrongful identification. Knuycky, Kleider, and Cavrak (2014) examined whether mistaken "familiarity" with prototypical Black faces would produce misidentifications. The researchers found that Black faces that were classified as stereotypically Black resulted in more identification errors than did non-stereotypical Black faces and produced a sense of (erroneous) familiarity. Hence, prototypicality can induce familiarity.

Osborne and Davies (2013) examined whether eyewitness identification accuracy is affected by stereotypes concerning a target's level of perceived stereotypicality across three studies. In Study 1, participants were shown a crime followed by a pair of mugshots. Participants were asked to decide which of the two targets committed the crime. The stereotypically Black crimes were drive-by shooting, gang-related beating, pimping, carjacking, cop killer, and street gambling; the stereotypically White crimes were internet hacker, insider trading, hate crime, identitity theft, embezzlement, and serial killer (Osborne & Davies, 2013). Participants selected the high perceived stereotypical target more often when the mugshots were paired with stereotypically Black crimes compared to stereotypically White crimes. Study 2 extended Study 1 such that participants were assigned to watch a video of a crime and were later asked to make an identification. Participants who expected to see a person suspected of a stereotypically Black crime (e.g., suspected pimp) recalled the target as being higher on perceived stereotypicality compared to those who expected to see the same person but who was suspected of a stereotypically White crime (e.g., suspected internet hacker) or a control event that depicted a man leaving a building who was not suspected of a specific crime. Last, Study 3 replicated Study 2 with the exception that new crimes were used that varied with regard to the stereotypes about the perpetrator's race (Osborne & Davies, 2013). Drive-by shooting and serial killer were used as a stereotypically Black crime and a stereotypically White crime, respectively. Only those participants who expected to see a person suspected of a stereotypically Black crime made inaccurate identifications. Taken together, these three studies show how stereotypes about certain races and crimes associated with those races can influence people's ability to accurately identify the perpetrator from a lineup. People's expectations and biases may promote "familiarity" that can result in memory errors.

What if your stereotype is not consistent with what you are experiencing? Kleider, Pezdek, Goldinger, and Kirk (2008) examined memory for photographs showing stereotype-consistent and stereotype-inconsistent actions. Participants watched a slideshow of a female and a male performing actions that were either gender-stereotype consistent or gender-stereotype inconsistent. Stereotype-consistent actions included using a wrench for the male and baking a cake for the female, whereas stereotype-inconsistent actions included the male baking a cake and the female using a wrench. Following a delay, participants were better able to recall actions that were stereotype consistent. When tested immediately, the recall was comparable between stereotype-consistent and stereotype-inconsistent actions. In addition, participants were asked to respond "remember" in cases in which they had conscious recollection of seeing the respective actor performing a specific action. Participants were more likely to inaccurately state they remembered when they were making stereotype-consistent errors. Kleider, Goldinger, and Knuycky's (2008) findings also support this, such that participants were likely to believe a behavior was present when, in fact, it was not when the behavior was stereotype consistent compared to stereotype inconsistent. These two studies suggest that stereotype consistency can hinder accuracy and that when people cannot accurately remember exactly what they saw, they may rely on their personally held stereotypes to fill in missing details, which may ultimately lead to an increase in false identifications or erroneous recall memory.

Stereotypes also may combine with familiarity to influence witness' recall of an event or person. For example, Cordón, Silberkleit, and Goodman (2016) found that children aged 4–5 and 7–9 years were significantly more likely to provide correct responses to free recall stereotype-related questions when the children were unfamiliar with the target person compared to when they were familiar with the target. In this study, participants were either introduced to the target prior to the identification task or not (i.e., prior exposure vs. no prior exposure). In addition, each target either matched a specific negative stereotype (i.e., depiction of a messy and clumsy individual) or did not. Approximately 2 weeks after the children in the familiar condition interacted with the target, they were subjected to a memory interview in which they were asked a series of free recall questions as well as a set of closed-ended questions. Familiarity improved the proportion of accurate identification responses, perhaps because the children had a longer exposure to the target. Interestingly, stereotypes lead children to answer close-ended questions with greater accuracy in general, but this effect was diminished when the children were asked more specific closed-ended questions about stereotype-related information (i.e., "Was Debbie messy or clean?"). Overall, Cordón and colleagues' (2016) results demonstrate that familiarity and stereotypes can interact and both enhance and hinder memory depending on the type of questions asked.

Other Ways in Which Familiarity Can Lead to Wrongful Conviction

As mentioned previously, mistaken identification is the leading cause of known wrongful convictions (see https://www.innocenceproject.org). Additional factors also have been found to contribute to wrongful conviction, such as false alibis, informants providing inaccurate information, prosecutorial misconduct, inadequate defense, false confessions, and faulty forensic science. How do these variables interact with defendant familiarity to influence conviction? We consider the factor of alibis.

Alibis from Familiar Others

A defendant may be asked to give an alibi as to where he or she was during the time a crime was committed. Of the first 157 DNA exonerations, more than 25% included an alibi provided by the defendant that was not believed (Burke, Turtle, & Olson, 2007). This disbelief in alibi may be because the person providing the alibi for the defendant was familiar to him or her. Those who share a highly familiar relationship (i.e., biological) are less likely to be believed because it is thought that they have more motivation to lie (Hosch, Culhane, Jolly, Chavez, & Shaw, 2011).

Culhane and Hosch (2004) examined whether the degree of familiarity shared between the defendant and alibi witness was influential in jurors' decisions, in addition to the type of alibi testimony and the eyewitness' confidence level. Mock jurors were less likely to convict the defendant when a neighbor testified compared to when the defendant's girlfriend testified, suggesting that even a non-intimate degree of familiarity is enough to lead jurors to question the honesty of the alibi. Hosch and colleagues (2011, Study 1) examined whether the degree of relatedness of the alibi witness to the defendant would influence jurors' decisions. The alibi witness was a twin brother, sister, half-sister, cousin, or second cousin. In addition, they included family members by marriage: the defendant's wife, his sister-in-law, his half sister-in-law, his cousin by marriage, and his second cousin by marriage. Last, non-kin alibi witnesses were examined: the defendant's oldest best friend, his co-worker, a neighbor, a person regularly seen at a store but not known by name, or a total stranger. Participants were more skeptical of the honesty of the alibi when the alibi witness and the defendant shared a biological relationship and least skeptical when the alibi witness and the defendant were not related. Interestingly, the degree of biological relationship also influenced perceptions of the alibi witness' credibility, such that the credibility increased when the degree of relatedness decreased (Hosch et al., 2011). Thus, familiarity as a function of alibi can also play a role in the wrongful conviction of an innocent person outside of eyewitness identification.

Conclusion

Our sense of familiarity can lead to misidentifying a perpetrator. At times, we may believe we see someone who is familiar, but this sense of familiarity may be incorrect in various ways. For example, you may identify someone who seems familiar, and indeed this person was present during the crime but was not the perpetrator. Alternatively, you may witness a perpetrator and think he or she is someone who you have seen in another context but it turns out that you are mistaken. Our familiarity errors can be a result of misattribution and source monitoring or even stereotyping. It is important to be aware of how a sense of familiarity can result in misidentification. Once we know about the influences that familiarity can exert and how familiarity can interact with other factors (both system and estimator variables; see Chapters 5 and 6, this volume), we are in a better position to try to prevent erroneous identifications.

References

Ainsworth, P. (1998). Turning heroes into villains: The role of unconscious transference in media crime reporting. In J. Boros, I. Münnich, & M. Szegedi (Eds.), *Psychology and criminal justice: International review of theory and practice: A publication of the European Association of Psychology and Law* (pp. 399–406). Berlin, Germany: de Gruyter.

Anderson, J. R., & Bower, G. H. (1972). Recognition and retrieval processes in free recall. *Psychological Review, 79*, 97–123.

Anderson, J. R., & Bower, G. H. (1974). A propositional theory of recognition memory. *Memory and Cognition, 2*, 406–412.

Brigham, J., & Cairns, D. (1988). The effect of mugshot inspections on eyewitness identification accuracy. *Journal of Applied Social Psychology, 18*, 1394–1410. doi:10.1111/j.1559-1816.1988.tb01214.x

Burke, T. M., Turtle, J. W., & Olson, E. A. (2007). Alibis in criminal investigations and trials. In M. P. Toglia, D. F., Ross, J. D. Read, & R. C. L. Lindsay (Eds.), *Handbook of eyewitness psychology. Vol. 1: Memory for events* (pp. 157–174). Mahwah, NJ: Erlbaum.

Cordón, I. M., Silberkleit, G., & Goodman, G. S. (2016). Getting to know you: Familiarity, stereotypes, and children's eyewitness memory. *Behavioral Sciences & the Law, 34*(1), 74–94.

Culhane, S. E., & Hosch, H. M. (2004). An alibi witness' influence on mock jurors' verdicts. *Journal of Applied Social Psychology, 34*, 1604–1616. doi:10.1111/j.1559-1816.2004.tb02789.x

Dysart, J., Lindsay, R., Hammond, R., & Dupius, P. (2001). Mug shot exposure prior to lineup identification: Interference, transference, and commitment effects. *Journal of Applied Psychology, 86*, 1280–1284.

Hosch, H. M., Culhane, S. E., Jolly, K. W., Chavez, R. M., & Shaw, L. H. (2011). Effects of an alibi witness's relationship to the defendant on mock jurors' judgments. *Law and Human Behavior, 35*, 127–142. doi:10.1007/s10979-010-9225-5

Johnson, M. K., Hashtroudi, S., & Lindsay, S. D. (1993). Source monitoring. *Psychological Bulletin, 114*, 3–28.

Johnson, M. K., & Raye, C. L. (1981). Reality monitoring. *Psychological Review, 88*, 67–85.

Kersten, A. W., & Earles, J. L. (2017). Feelings of familiarity and false memory for specific associations resulting from mugshot exposure. *Memory & Cognition, 45*(1), 93–104.

Kersten, A. W., Earles, J., & Upshaw, C. (2013). False recollection of the role played by an actor in an event. *Memory & Cognition, 41*(8), 1144–1158.

Kleider, H. M., Goldinger, S. D., & Knuycky, L. (2008). Stereotypes influence false memories for imagined events. *Memory, 16*(2), 97–114.

Kleider, H. M., Pezdek, K., Goldinger, S. D., & Kirk, A. (2008). Schema-driven source misattribution errors: Remembering the expected from a witnessed event. *Applied Cognitive Psychology, 22*(1), 1–20.

Knuycky, L. R., Kleider, H. M., & Cavrak, S. E. (2014). Line-up misidentifications: When being "prototypically Black" is perceived as criminal. *Applied Cognitive Psychology, 28*(1), 39–46.

Lamson, N., & Behrman, B. (1997). The biasing effect of the photographic showup compared to the lineup on later lineup identification. *Proceedings of the Human Factors and Ergonomics Society Annual Meeting, 41*, 538–542.

Loftus, E. F. (1976). Unconscious transference in eyewitness identification. *Law and Psychological Review, 2*, 93–98.

Meissner, C., & Brigham, J. (2001). Thirty years of investigating the own-race bias in memory for faces: A meta-analytic review. *Psychology, Public Policy, and Law, 7*(1), 3–35. doi:10.1037/1076-8971.7.1.3

Memon, A., Hope, L., Bartlett, J., & Bull, R. (2002). Eyewitness recognition errors: The effects of mugshot viewing and choosing in young and old adults. *Memory and Cognition, 30*, 1219–1227.

Memon, A., Hope, L., & Bull, R. (2003). Exposure duration: Effects on eyewitness accuracy and confidence. *British Journal of Psychology, 94*, 339–354. doi:10.1348.000712603767876262

Mitchell, K. J., Johnson, M. K., & Mather, M. (2003). Source monitoring and suggestibility to misinformation: Adult age-related differences. *Applied Cognitive Psychology, 17*, 107–119.

Osborne, D., & Davies, P. (2013). Eyewitness identifications are affected by stereotypes about a suspect's level of perceived stereotypicality. *Group Processes and Intergroup Relations, 16*(4), 488–504.

Read, J., Tollestrup, P., Hammersley, R., McFadzen, E., & Christensen, A. (1990). The unconscious transference effect: Are innocent bystanders ever misidentified? *Applied Cognitive Psychology, 4*, 3–31.

Ross, D., Ceci, S., Dunning, D., & Toglia, M. (1994). Unconscious transference and mistaken identity: When a witness misidentifies a familiar but innocent person. *Journal of Applied Psychology, 79*, 918–930.

Ross, D., Marsil, D., Benton, T., Hoffman, R., Warren, A., Lindsay, R., & Metzger, R. (2006). Children's susceptibility to misidentifying a familiar bystander from a lineup: When younger is better. *Law and Human Behavior, 30*, 249–257. doi:10.1007/s10979-006-9034-z

The National Registry of Exonerations. (2017). *Joseph Lamont Abbitt*. Retrieved November 4, 2017, from https://www.law.umich.edu/special/exoneration/Pages/casedetail.aspx?caseid=3807

8

How Persuasive Is an Eyewitness Who Is Familiar with the Defendant?

In previous chapters, we discussed theories of familiarity and factors that can combine with familiarity to influence an eyewitness' recall and identification accuracy. Factors that can influence eyewitness identification are also often present in the courtroom, where the defendant is put on trial and is judged by a jury of his or her peers. We also have discussed cases in which familiarity has played a role and how familiarity can ultimately lead to a wrongful conviction of an innocent person. Jurors can be influenced by a number of different factors. Eyewitness identification has been found to be one of the most persuasive types of evidence presented to the jury (Brewer & Wells, 2011). However, the majority of research examining jurors' decisions uses the identification of a stranger.

Researchers have found that jurors have difficulty distinguishing between accurate and inaccurate eyewitnesses, with jurors typically believing eyewitnesses are accurate more than they are inaccurate (Lindsay, Wells, & Rumpel, 1981). Given these conclusions are based on research that has focused primarily on stranger identifications, one could speculate that an eyewitness who claims to be familiar with the defendant could be even more persuasive to jurors. In addition, many variables have been found to influence jurors' perceptions of an eyewitness' identification of a stranger. For example, eyewitness age has been shown to be influential, such that older eyewitnesses (e.g., those aged 12 years or older) are typically perceived more favorably than younger eyewitnesses (e.g., those aged 10 years or younger; Bruer & Pozzulo, 2014; Pozzulo 2016). Gender also has been shown to be influential in the context of a juror's gender, a defendant's gender, and an eyewitness' gender. For example, research often finds that female jurors are more

Familiarity and Conviction in the Criminal Justice System. Joanna Pozzulo, Emily Pica, and Chelsea Sheahan, Oxford University Press (2020). © Oxford University Press
DOI: 10.1093/oso/9780190874810.001.0001

pro-victim than are male jurors (Forsterlee, Forsterlee, Horowitz, & King, 2006; Pozzulo, Dempsey, Maeder, & Allen, 2010; Wayne, Riordan, & Thomas, 2001). Typically, studies that examine juror decision-making include various independent variables to determine whether familiarity can influence more than one variable. Thus, how familiarity influences judgments of guilt and perceptions of the eyewitness and/or defendant is discussed in this chapter.

Familiarity Operationalizations and Juror Decision-Making

As mentioned in Chapter 1, there is no clear-cut definition of familiarity. Although the dictionary defines *familiarity* as reasonable knowledge or acquaintance, as with a subject or place ("Familiarity," 2013), that does not always translate to the research setting. For example, how does one measure "reasonable knowledge" or "acquaintance" with a subject or place? Qualitatively what does this mean? Quantitatively what does this mean? To date, three primary operationalizations of familiarity have been used: exposure duration, number of exposures, and relationship (Lindsay, Lim, Marando, & Cully, 1986; Pica, Sheahan, Mesesan, & Pozzulo, 2017; Pozzulo, Pettalia, Bruer, & Javaid, 2014). Juror decision-making studies include different measures (i.e., perceptions of guilt, witness credibility, etc.) to determine whether familiarity can influence more than one factor. Thus, how familiarity influences judgments of guilt and perceptions of the eyewitness and/or defendant is discussed next.

Exposure Duration

Perhaps one of the first studies to examine the notion of familiarity in a juror context is that by Lindsay and colleagues (1986), who examined the influence of exposure duration on mock jurors' judgments. This study used audiotapes to present a mock trial to participants. Although the study did not set out to examine familiarity specifically, the results can be extrapolated. Recall from previous chapters that exposure duration is often used to manipulate "familiarity." Participants heard a case concerning a mock burglary in which the eyewitness had less than a 5-second exposure to the perpetrator, a 30-minute exposure to the perpetrator, or a 30-minute exposure to the perpetrator with interaction. There was no influence of exposure duration on jurors' guilt judgments. When the eyewitness viewed the defendant for less than 5 seconds, jurors perceived the eyewitness to have significantly less opportunity to view the perpetrator compared to the eyewitness with the longer exposures. This suggests that although jurors may take exposure duration into account when considering the facts of the case, it is not obvious how this will transfer to verdict decision. However, Lindsay and colleagues did find that those who voted guilty listed interaction (or lack thereof) as one of their reasons.

Number of Exposures

Another common manipulation for familiarity is the number of exposures to the perpetrator. Pozzulo and colleagues (2014) examined whether this would influence mock jurors' judgments. Participants read a mock trial transcript concerning a murder. The eyewitness reported seeing the perpetrator zero, three, or six times prior to the commission of the crime. In addition, eyewitness age was varied in different versions of the transcript so that the eyewitness was 4, 12, or 20 years old. There was no influence of familiarity on jurors' judgments, nor was there a combined influence of eyewitness age and familiarity on jurors' judgments. However, Pozzulo and colleagues included follow-up questions regarding how many exposures to a person would produce an accurate identification. The majority of participants suggested three times was sufficient for an accurate identification, followed by only seeing the person once, six times, and seven or more times, respectively.

Sheahan, Pozzulo, Reed, and Pica (2017) examined whether the number of exposures to the perpetrator was likely to sway mock juror decision-making. Participants were presented with a trial transcript in which the eyewitness saw the perpetrator zero or eight times while shopping at a convenience store. Sheahan and colleagues found that mock jurors were more likely to vote guilty and assign higher guilt ratings for the defendant (i.e., assessing the defendant's guilt on a continuous scale of 0 [not at all guilty] to 100 [very guilty]) when the eyewitness testified that she saw him at the convenience store eight times compared to never seeing him prior to the commission of the crime. The number of exposures, however, did not influence mock jurors' perceptions of the eyewitness. Sheahan and colleagues speculated that their stronger manipulation of familiarity may be one reason they found an effect of familiarity while Pozzulo and colleagues (2014) did not. In addition, Pozzulo and colleagues portrayed the defendant as a mail carrier, whereas Sheahan and colleagues described the defendant as a convenience store clerk with whom the eyewitness spoke on each of the eight occasions. The role the defendant played could have influenced how mock jurors perceived the shared familiarity with the eyewitness.

Taken together, these studies that operationalize familiarity in terms of prior exposure, or exposure time, suggest that exposure may not be sufficient to influence jurors' overall perceptions of the eyewitness. Based on these studies, it appears that seeing someone eight times and interacting with the person is enough perceived familiarity between an eyewitness and a defendant for mock jurors to believe the eyewitness made an accurate identification. However, as evidenced in Chapter 1, the prior exposure that the eyewitness had with the defendant can also backfire, as in the case of William Snyder. In this case, the witness remembered seeing Snyder before, as the eyewitness believed he was her neighbor, and erroneously inferred that he was the perpetrator.

Context of Relationship

Recently, researchers have begun to examine whether the relationship shared between the eyewitness and the perpetrator influences mock jurors' judgments. Familiarity, in this context, is typically varied between a complete stranger, an acquaintance, or a well-known person. For example, Pica and colleagues (2017) examined familiarity in the context of relationships across three studies. The first study varied the relationship between the defendant and the eyewitness, such that the shared relationship was between a teacher and a student, a lunch monitor and a student, or strangers. In addition, the delay between the crime and identification was varied. Familiarity did influence mock jurors' continuous guilt ratings, such that when the defendant was the eyewitness' former teacher, he received higher guilt ratings compared to if the defendant and eyewitness were strangers. Also, familiarity combined with identification delay such that when there was either a 1-week or a 1-year delay from when the identification was made, the defendant received higher guilt ratings when he was the eyewitness' former teacher or lunch monitor compared to a stranger. The second study varied familiarity in terms of relationship such that the defendant and eyewitness shared a biological relationship (uncle), social relationship (lunch monitor), or no relationship (stranger). Similar to the first study, mock jurors were more likely to assign higher guilt ratings to the defendant if he was the eyewitness' uncle compared to if he was a stranger. Pica and colleagues' third study varied familiarity between neighbor and stranger and found no differences between the neighbor and the stranger in terms of defendant guilt. These three studies support the notion that mock jurors may take the relationship shared between the defendant and the eyewitness into account when rendering a guilt judgment. It appears that when the defendant and eyewitness share either a familial or a personal relationship, such as between a teacher and a student, mock jurors believe that the relationship warrants enough familiarity that the eyewitness would be able to make an accurate identification.

Pozzulo, Sheahan, and Pratt (2019) examined familiarity in the context of social relationships such that the eyewitness and defendant shared a familiar relationship in which the defendant was the eyewitness' teacher, an acquaintance relationship in which the defendant was the eyewitness' pizza delivery person, or they were complete strangers. In addition, the age of the eyewitness (5, 10, or 15 years old) and type of crime (personal or nonpersonal) were varied. Pica and colleagues found that jurors were more likely to assign higher guilt ratings to the defendant when he shared a familiar relationship with the eyewitness and the crime was personal (i.e., an abduction). In addition, mock jurors were more likely to believe the eyewitness made an accurate identification when the crime was an abduction and the defendant was the eyewitness' teacher or pizza delivery person compared to a stranger. Pica and colleagues found that even social, familiar relationships can influence mock jurors.

Clearly, familiarity plays a role in how jurors perceive an eyewitness and his or her identification of the defendant. However, the results have been inconsistent throughout the literature, thus suggesting that familiarity needs to be further examined. The two most common operationalizations of familiarity in the context of juror decision-making thus far have been number of exposures and relationship. The question remains, however, when does the number of exposures translate into a relationship? Moreover, how many exposures does it take to form a relationship? Is "interaction" necessary for it to be considered a relationship? Should the nature of the interaction be considered?

It is important to examine how the strength of a shared relationship between the eyewitness and the perpetrator influences mock jurors' decision-making because as discussed in Chapter 1, a man could be misidentified as a family member and then wrongfully convicted for a crime he or she did not commit, similar to what happened to Clarence Elkins when he was erroneously identified as the perpetrator because the victim believed the perpetrator looked like her uncle.

Familiarity and Eyewitness Confidence

In *Neil v. Biggers* (1972), the US Supreme Court identified five criteria on which judging eyewitness evidence should be based: the opportunity of the witness to view the criminal during the crime, the witness' degree of attention, the accuracy of the witness' description of the criminal, the level of certainty demonstrated by the eyewitness at the time of confrontation, and the length of time between the crime and confrontation (p. 199). Given that an eyewitness' confidence is associated with these five criteria, it is important to examine (1) how eyewitness confidence and familiarity influence jurors and (2) under what circumstances a confident witness will be more or less influential in jurors' decisions.

Confidence can be conceptualized as the strength of a memory match between the eyewitness' memory for the perpetrator and the lineup photograph selected (Sauer & Brewer, 2015). When confidence is high, it can be assumed that the memory match is strong. Early researchers who examined the influence of an eyewitness' confidence found that the level of confidence was highly influential in determining a witness' credibility (Lindsay et al., 1981; Wells, Lindsay, & Tousignant, 1980). These results have remained steady during the past several decades, such that researchers are still finding that confident eyewitnesses are more influential in jurors' decisions than are non-confident witnesses. For example, in a study by Brewer and Burke (2002), participants listened to an audiotaped trial depicting an armed robbery. The eyewitness displayed high or low confidence and provided either a consistent statement or a statement with some inconsistencies. Brewer and Burke found that an eyewitness who displays high confidence is typically perceived as being more accurate than an eyewitness who displays low confidence; however, testimonial inconsistencies had no impact. When an eyewitness is familiar with the perpetrator, his or her confidence in the identification task may be even more elevated compared to when the eyewitness may make a stranger identification. As such, it can be expected that a highly confident, familiar eyewitness would be more persuasive to a jury compared to a highly confident, unfamiliar eyewitness.

Vallano, Pettalia, Pica, and Pozzulo (2019) examined prior exposure in conjunction with eyewitness confidence to determine whether they influenced mock jurors' judgments. Familiarity varied between seeing the defendant once prior to the crime and seeing the defendant many times prior to the crime. Although there were no significant results, there was a trend for familiar identifications to be perceived as more accurate and indicative of guilt compared to stranger identifications, but only when the eyewitness had seen the defendant once prior to the crime. Vallano and colleagues also asked mock jurors whether they believed familiar identifications would be more accurate than stranger identifications, and more than half of them believed that they would be more accurate. Furthermore, approximately 70% of participants believed that an eyewitness would be more accurate in his or her identification when the eyewitness had seen the perpetrator many times prior to the crime compared to only seeing the perpetrator once prior to the crime. These results are intriguing because participants were more likely to believe that an identification of a familiar person would be more accurate than an identification of a stranger, but this did not significantly impact their decisions concerning defendant culpability. This supports the notion that laypeople do not fully comprehend factors that impact eyewitness identification.

Pica, Sheahan, Pozzulo, Vallano, and Pettalia (2018) examined the combined influence of eyewitness age, familiarity with the defendant, and the eyewitness' confidence on jurors' decisions across three studies. In the first study, Pica and colleagues did not find an effect of familiarity nor a combined effect of familiarity and confidence. The authors suggested that it may be because the degree of familiarity shared between the eyewitness and defendant did not include any interaction (e.g., a conversation). Therefore, they conducted a second study that examined familiarity in the context of interactions and confidence. For example, the eyewitness was described as having talked to the defendant many times or only once while shopping in a store at the mall. However, this was not enough to warrant the sense of familiarity because only eyewitness confidence played a role in jurors' judgments. Given that a vague description of exposures (i.e., many times or once) was not enough to influence jurors, Pica and colleagues conducted a third study in which the number of exposures was explicitly mentioned (0 vs. 10 vs. 20 times). Familiarity did influence mock jurors' beliefs regarding whether the identification was accurate such that when the eyewitness reported seeing the defendant 10 times prior to the crime compared to never having seen the defendant, mock jurors believed the identification was accurate. There was also a combined influence of familiarity and confidence such that when the eyewitness saw the defendant 20 times prior to the crime and reported having high confidence, mock jurors were more likely to believe the identification was accurate compared to when the eyewitness reported low confidence.

Pettalia, Pica, Pratt, and Pozzulo (2019) took a different approach and examined familiarity in the context of relationships. The defendant was portrayed as the eyewitness' father, the eyewitness' mother's boyfriend, or a stranger. Familiarity did influence jurors' decisions such that when the eyewitness and defendant shared a familial relationship or when the defendant was the eyewitness' mother's boyfriend, jurors were more likely to find the defendant guilty. However, confidence did not play a role with the degree of familiarity possibly because only two levels of confidence were examined (50% vs. 100% confident). Also, given that confidence can be subjective, numerical representations of confidence may mean different things to different people and may not be as clear-cut as "high" or "low" confidence.

There are several cases in which eyewitnesses display confidence in their identification that involves a "familiar" defendant. In one such case, a moderately confident witness testified that resulted in a wrongful conviction. Jimmy Ray Bromgard was charged and convicted of three counts of sexual intercourse without consent (Innocence Project, 2019). Bromgard was 18 years old when he went to prison and spent 14 years in prison for a crime he did not commit, based in part on eyewitness testimony. The eyewitness testified that she was 60–65% confident that Bromgard was her assailant. Keep in mind that her confidence level was just slightly more than chance. However, this level of confidence was enough to persuade jurors that her identification may be accurate.

Overall, the combination of familiarity and confidence does have the potential to be influential to mock jurors (Vallano et al., 2019), but results across studies are contradictory. Much more research needs to be conducted examining jurors' perceptions of an eyewitness' confidence when he or she identifies a familiar person because confidence level is typically recorded after an eyewitness makes an identification and can be influenced by other eyewitness or case variables.

Familiarity and the Courts

Familiarity between the defendant and the eyewitness has made its way into the courtroom. In previous years, the courts tended to subscribe to the notion that factors that may influence eyewitness identification are "common sense" to jurors (Benton, Ross, Bradshaw, Thomas, & Bradshaw, 2006). It took several years for the courts to allow expert testimony concerning eyewitness identification to be permitted (Fishman & Loftus, 1978). One such case in which the inclusion of expert testimony was allowed was *State v. Robinson* (1991), in which the defendant was charged with first-degree murder and robbery with a dangerous weapon. Although the defendant was ultimately convicted of both charges, the judge did allow the defense to call an expert to discuss the fallibility of eyewitness identification, especially when a weapon is present (i.e., the weapon-focus effect, as discussed in Chapter 6, this volume) and the defendant and eyewitness are of different races (i.e., cross-race effect; see Chapter 6, this volume). With research moving to include familiarity manipulations to mimic the reality of actual crime (note that most crime is committed by someone "familiar" to the victim; e.g., Flowe, Mehta, & Ebbesen, 2011; Memon, Havard, Clifford, Gabbert, & Wyatt, 2011), it is important to review cases wherein familiarity with the defendant was claimed.

Flowe and colleagues (2011) reported that in approximately half of criminal trials, the eyewitness is familiar with the defendant. An early example of how familiarity can play a role in the court can be seen in the appeal of *Bowlin v. Commonwealth* (1922), whereby the court stated that "hence a witness who identified the defendant as the criminal by his voice, with which the witness was familiar, and who could not recognize the defendant because it was dark, may, nevertheless be considered an eyewitness" (Higdon, 1923, p. 600). The mere familiarity of the defendant's voice was enough for the court to determine that the person could be considered an eyewitness. In *People v. Collins* (1983), the judge ruled,

> When a crime has been committed by a family member, former friend or long-time acquaintance of a witness, there is little or no risk that comments by police, however suggestive, will lead the witness to identify the wrong person. But in cases where the prior relationship is fleeting or distant it would be unrealistic to ignore the possibility that police suggestion may improperly influence the witness in making an identification.

This ruling is troublesome because research has reliably demonstrated that even changing just one word in a question can influence how eyewitnesses respond to the question (Loftus & Palmer, 1974). This ruling places an overconfidence on familiar persons, and as discussed in Chapter 1, familiarity can often backfire and lead to wrongful convictions. Interestingly, no research has examined the influence of suggestibility and familiarity in eyewitness identification; this is one avenue that future research should explore to determine the veracity of the judge's ruling.

The ruling in *People v. Collins* (1983) also came into play on appeal in the case of *The State of Kansas v. Mitchell* (2009) nearly 30 years later. A sole eyewitness, who also was the victim, identified Mitchell as a perpetrator in an aggravated robbery case. The eyewitness stated that he was familiar with Mitchell because they had met months before and the man actually stayed in his apartment. However, the caveat was that he could not remember the perpetrator's name. Police also reported that there had been a prior confrontation between the same two men in the same location, after which the eyewitness gave a description of the attacker. This description was then discovered to match the current description of the attacker, which is what led police to Mitchell. When shown the photo lineup, the eyewitness was 100% confident in his selection of the defendant. The defense appealed that the cautionary eyewitness instruction should have been used, which informs jurors of the factors that can influence the reliability of an eyewitness' identification. The court denied this motion, stating that "the cautionary eyewitness identification instruction is not required when the witness was personally familiar with the defendant because there is not a substantial likelihood of misidentification"; as such, the conviction was upheld. This is troublesome because the cautionary eyewitness instruction, known as the Telfaire instruction, alerts jurors to potential pitfalls of eyewitness evidence (*U.S. v. Telfaire*, 1972). This ruling, similar to the ruling discussed previously, places overconfidence on familiar identifications.

More recently, Vallano and Winter (2016) discussed the case of *State v. Williams* (2013), in which the eyewitness claimed to be familiar with the defendant because he was a regular customer of hers. The defense wanted to include expert testimony to discuss the fallibility of eyewitness memory and how identification errors can occur. However, the judge denied this request, stating that in cases of familiar identifications, the possibility of a misidentification is too low to warrant allowing an expert to testify (Vallano & Winter, 2016). After appeal, the Connecticut Supreme Court agreed and stated that because the eyewitness was familiar to the defendant, expert testimony would not be helpful to the jury.

There may be some instances in which expert testimony may not be needed with regard to familiarity. For example, consider the case of *State v. Guilbert* (2012). There were four eyewitnesses who had known the perpetrator for many years, and each eyewitness identified the same man. When there is this much evidence of a suspect's guilt, perhaps expert testimony is not warranted. However, what about those eyewitnesses who have seen the perpetrator in passing, but on a regular basis?

More recently, there is the case of *State v. Salmond* (personal communication with Lisa Steele, November 30, 2017), in which the eyewitness claimed he was familiar with the defendant. The eyewitness claimed that he had seen the defendant in a cell phone video and recognized him from "seeing him around" once or twice a week for roughly 2 weeks prior to the crime. However, suggestive procedures were used during the identification process; the detectives even went so far as to show the eyewitness the surveillance video of the crime prior to showing him the photo array. Once the eyewitness identified Salmond, the detectives' reactions confirmed to the eyewitness that this is who they wanted him to pick. This also could establish a sense of familiarity, as mentioned in Chapter 2, due to prior exposure.

Interestingly, in Massachusetts, familiarity has been defined as being measured by factors such as the number of times the witness viewed the suspect previously; the duration, nature, and setting of those encounters; and the period of time during which the encounters occurred (personal communication, November 30, 2017). This can be problematic because previous research has shown that depending on the number of previous exposures, jurors may not be influenced by the level of familiarity shared between the defendant and the eyewitness. Courts may need to be informed of the data being collected on the topic.

Conclusion

Although the results are somewhat inconsistent, possibly due to the lack of a common operationalization of familiarity, familiar identifications can impact jurors' judgments. In addition, as evidenced by prior court rulings, familiarity also has the potential to influence a judge's ruling. This is troublesome given that the research on the influence of familiarity on eyewitness identification accuracy is still in its infancy and the answer may not be as "obvious" as common sense.

References

Benton, T., Ross, D., Bradshaw, E., Thomas W., & Bradshaw, G. (2006). Eyewitness memory is still not common sense: Comparing jurors, judges, and law enforcement to eyewitness experts. *Applied Cognitive Psychology, 20*, 115–129. doi:10.1002/acp.1171

Bowlin v. Commonwealth, 195 KY, 600, 242 S.W. 604 (1922).

Brewer, N., & Burke, A. (2002). Effects of testimonial inconsistencies and eyewitness confidence on mock-juror judgments. *Law and Human Behavior, 26*(3), 353–364. doi:http://dx.doi.org/10.1023/A:1015380522722

Brewer, N., & Wells, G. (2011). Eyewitness identification. *Current Directions in Psychological Science, 20*, 24–27. doi:10.1177/0963721410389169

Bruer, K., & Pozzulo, J. D. (2014). Influence of eyewitness age and recall error on mock juror decision-making. *Legal and Criminological Psychology, 19*(2), 332–348. doi:10.1111/lcrp.12001

Familiarity. (2013). *Collins English Dictionary*. Retrieved January 24, 2019, from http://www.collinsdictionary.com/dictionary/english/familiarity?showCookiePolicy=true

Fishman, D. B., & Loftus, E. F. (1978). Expert testimony on eyewitness identification. *Law and Psychology Review, 4*, 87–103.

Flowe, H. D., Mehta, A., & Ebbesen, E. (2011). The role of eyewitness identification evidence in felony case dispositions. *Psychology, Public Policy, and Law, 17*(1), 140–159. doi:10.1037/a0021311

Forsterlee, R., Forsterlee, L., Horowitz, I., & King, E. (2006). The effects of defendant race, victim race, and juror gender on evidence processing in a murder trial. *Behavioral Sciences and the Law, 24*, 179–198. doi:10.1002/bsl.675

Higdon, R. G. (1923). *Civil and criminal cases decided by the court of appeals of Kentucky* (Vol. 195). Frankfort, KY: The State Journal Company.

Innocence Project. (2019). *Jimmy Ray Bromgard*. Retrieved January 23, 2019, from https://www.innocenceproject.org/cases/jimmy-ray-bromgard

Lindsay, R. C. L., Lim, R., Marando, L., & Cully D. (1986). Mock-juror evaluations of eyewitness testimony: A test of metamemory hypotheses. *Journal of Applied Social Psychology, 16*, 447–459. doi:10.1111/j.1559-1816.1986.tb01151.x

Lindsay, R. C. L., Wells, G. L., & Rumpel, C. M. (1981). Can people detect eyewitness-identification accuracy within and across situations? *Journal of Applied Psychology, 66*(1), 79–89. doi:10.1037/0021-9010.66.1.79

Loftus, E., & Palmer, J. (1974). Reconstruction of automobile destruction: An example of the interaction between language and memory. *Journal of Verbal Learning and Verbal Behavior, 13*, 585–589.

Memon, A., Havard, C., Clifford, B., Gabbert, F., & Wyatt, M. (2011). A field evaluation of the VIPER system: A new technique for eliciting eyewitness identification evidence. *Psychology, Crime & Law, 17*, 711–729. doi:10.1080/10683160903524333

Neil v. Biggers, 409 US 188 (1972).

People v. Collins, 143 Cal. App. 3d 742, 192 (1983).

Pettalia, J., Pica, E., Pratt, K., & Pozzulo, J. (2019). *Characteristics of a credible witness: Consistency, confidence, and familiarity with the defendant.* Submitted for publication.

Pica, E., Pozzulo, J., Sheahan, C., & Pratt, K. (2019). *"I know him!": Does witness–defendant familiarity impact mock jurors across different aged witnesses and types of crime?* Submitted for publication.

Pica, E., Sheahan, C., Mesesan, A., & Pozzulo, J. (2017). The influence of prior familiarity, identification delay, appearance change, and descriptor type on mock jurors' judgments. *Journal of Police and Criminal Psychology, 33*(4), 289–301. doi:https://doi.org/10.1007/s11896-017-9251-z

Pica, E., Sheahan, C. L., Pozzulo, J., Vallano, J., & Pettalia, J. (2018). The influence of familiar and confident eyewitnesses on mock jurors' judgments. *Journal of Police and Criminal Psychology*. Advance Online Publication. doi: 10.1007/s11896-018-9306-9

Pozzulo, J. D. (2016). *Describing and identifying perpetrators: The young eyewitness*. Washington, DC: American Psychological Association.

Pozzulo, J. D., Dempsey, J., Maeder, E., & Allen, L. (2010). The effects of victim gender, defendant gender, and defendant age on juror decision making. *Criminal Justice and Behavior, 37*, 47–63. doi:10.1177/0093854809344173

Pozzulo, J. D., Pettalia, J. L., Bruer, K., & Javaid, S. (2014). Eyewitness age and familiarity with the defendant: Influential factors in mock jurors' assessments of defendant guilt. *American Journal of Forensic Psychology, 32*, 39–51.

Sauer, J. D., & Brewer, N. (2015). Confidence and accuracy of eyewitness identification. In T. Valentine & J. P. Davis (Eds.), *Forensic facial identification: Theory and practice of identification from eyewitnesses, composites, and CCTV* (pp. 185–208). Hoboken, NJ: Wiley.

Sheahan, C., Pozzulo, J., Reed, J., & Pica, E. (2017). The role of familiarity with the defendant, type of descriptor discrepancy, and eyewitness age on mock jurors' perceptions of eyewitness testimony. *Journal of Police and Criminal Psychology, 33*, 35–44.

State v. Guilbert, 306 Conn. 218, 49 A.3d 705 (2012).

State v. Mitchell, No. 99,163, 2009 WL 311814, at *3-4 (Kan. App. 2009) (unpublished opinion).

State v. Robinson, 330 N.C. 1 (1991).

State v. Williams, 146 Conn. App. 114, 116-17, 75 A.3d 668 (2013).

U.S. v. Telfaire, 469 F. 2d 522, 558-559 (1972).

Vallano, J. P., Pettalia, J., Pica, E., & Pozzulo, J. (2019). An examination of mock jurors' judgments in familiar identification cases. *Journal of Police and Criminal Psychology, 34*(2), 121–133. doi:https://doi.org/10.1007/s11896-018-9266-0

Vallano, J. P., & Winter, R. J. (2016). I think I've seen you before: How should courts deal with expert witness testimony when the eyewitness may have seen the perpetrator before the crime? *Judicial Notebook, 47*(5), 26.

Wayne, J. H., Riordan, C. M., & Thomas, K. M. (2001). Is all sexual harassment viewed the same? Mock juror decisions in same- and cross-gender cases. *Journal of Applied Psychology, 86*(2), 179–187. doi:10.1037/0021-9010.86.2.179

Wells, G. L., Lindsay, R., & Tousignant, J. (1980). Effects of expert psychological advice on human performance in judging the validity of eyewitness testimony. *Law and Human Behavior, 4*, 275–285. doi:10.1007/BF01040619

9

Future Directions for Research Examining the Notion of Familiarity and Its Impact on the Criminal Justice System

This book is an effort to consolidate the research on "familiarity" with a perpetrator in an eyewitness context. We have provided the various conceptualizations of familiarity along with paradigms used to assess the impact of familiarity on eyewitness testimony. We explored two broad domains, namely cognitive and social psychology, that have relevant research on the topic to provide an understanding on how we should evaluate eyewitness testimony when the eyewitness declares "familiarity" with the perpetrator. We also explored how jurors may interpret these declarations. In this chapter, we discuss how researchers may want to move forward as we try to develop best practices for collecting and evaluating familiar eyewitness testimony.

Why Has Familiar-Stranger Identification Largely Been Ignored Until Now?

To date, the vast majority of eyewitness research has focused on describing and identifying a stranger who has committed a crime. From the research examining perpetrators who are strangers, we have learned how memory can be influenced and the best practices that can be used to increase accuracy. In Chapter 1, and in various chapters throughout this book, many cases were highlighted that involved some level of perceived familiarity shared between the eyewitness and the perpetrator. Moreover, research has found that in the

Familiarity and Conviction in the Criminal Justice System. Joanna Pozzulo, Emily Pica, and Chelsea Sheahan, Oxford University Press (2020). © Oxford University Press
DOI: 10.1093/oso/9780190874810.001.0001

majority of crimes that are committed, the eyewitness or victim has some degree of familiarity with the perpetrator (Miethe & Drass, 1999). Research matching the reality of real-life crime has been ignored for the most part. Perhaps the main reason for the focus on stranger identification is the perception that this scenario provides the most informative evidence. For example, if a witness declares he or she "knows" the assaulter, identification is less critical. The witness can inform police who is the perpetrator. The messiness of defining the term, operationalizing it, and developing appropriate paradigms to measure the various degrees of familiarity all present challenges to investigating the topic. The small number of studies that have been conducted on familiarity indicate that the relationship between the broad notion of familiarity and identification is not straightforward, at times having no influence on accuracy, under some conditions improving accuracy, and at other times perhaps leading to inaccuracy. Understanding the impact of familiarity on eyewitness identification is crucial given the likelihood of shared familiarity between an eyewitness or victim and a perpetrator.

Where Is the Field in Terms of Studying Familiarity?

Theme 1

Evident in virtually all the chapters of this book is the fact that there is a limited amount of research on the topic of familiarity. As mentioned previously, unfortunately, the majority of real-life cases involve a familiar-stranger identification (Miethe & Drass, 1999). There are a number of wrongful conviction cases in which the eyewitness claimed to be familiar with the perpetrator (see https://www.innocenceproject.org). It is important to note that claims of familiarity also can be accurate, such as in the case of Elizabeth Smart (for a description, see Chapter 1, this volume). We need to start teasing apart the conditions or factors that may give rise to a sense of familiarity and then investigate the factors that increase and decrease the likelihood of accurate eyewitness memories when familiarity may be present. How do we define, quantify, and operationalize what we mean by familiarity? Is it the amount of contact? Quality of contact? Is a certain degree of both elements required? Other elements?

We need to design paradigms that allow us to manipulate familiarity and then test its influence on variables that occur in real life. In all likelihood, familiarity will interact with both system (i.e., variables under the control of the criminal justice system) and estimator variables (i.e., those that occur at the time of the crime; Wells, 1978). Research across both types of variables is critical.

Theme 2

Turning to system variables, we may want to focus on the police practices or procedures that exacerbate errors when the possibility of familiarity with the perpetrator arises. Of course, unbiased and neutral interviewing protocols and lineup identification procedures should be used. However, do best practices differ if there is a possible issue of familiarity? It is critical to collect data on police procedures as a function of familiarity. There is a long-standing debate in the literature concerning which lineup procedure, simultaneous or sequential, is more effective (Gronlund, Carlson, Dailey, & Goodsell, 2009; Steblay, Dysart, & Wells, 2015; Wells, Dysart, & Steblay, 2015). Since the seminal work of Lindsay and Wells (1985) that investigated the novel approach of presenting a lineup sequentially (e.g., one photo at a time requiring an identification decision for each photo before moving ahead in the sequence), a vibrant debate has occurred on lineup procedures and their influence on identification accuracy. The past 30 years of research on lineup procedures has focused almost exclusively on stranger identifications. It is time to investigate lineup procedures when a perpetrator may be familiar. To date, only one study has examined the simultaneous–sequential debate with the familiar-stranger. Sheahan and Pozzulo (2019) found that the sequential superiority effect—that is, the sequential procedure produces a lower rate of correct identification and a higher rate of correct rejection compared to the simultaneous procedure, which produces a higher rate of correct identification and a lower rate of correct rejection—is essentially nullified when the eyewitness and perpetrator are familiar with each other. Sheahan and Pozzulo found that when the eyewitness was familiar with the perpetrator, high rates of correct identifications were found when using the sequential procedure, whereas high rates of correct rejections were found when using the simultaneous procedure. Further research is needed to examine the simultaneous–sequential debate with familiar identifications. If one procedure appears to be better with a suspected case of familiarity, it may tip the recommendation for best practice.

Similarly, it is important to consider the interview protocols used with eyewitness/victims when a familiar suspect is "suspected." Again, it appears common sense that investigators need to maintain a nonbiased approach with open-ended questioning in interviewing to ascertain who may be the perpetrator. The cognitive interview, for example, may be beneficial (for more on the cognitive interview, see Fisher & Geiselman, 1992) regardless of suspected level of familiarity between the eyewitness and the perpetrator. Data are required, however, before definitive conclusions can be made recommending one protocol over another in cases of suspected familiarity. Does the type of questioning change if there is a suspected familiar suspect?

Theme 3

A number of estimator variables (along with system variables) may interact with familiarity. Several common estimator variables in several real-life cases, including familiarity, involve the age of the eyewitness/victim, cross-race identification, type of crime (e.g., violent vs. nonviolent), and, relatedly, role as either eyewitness or victim. It is not obvious whether a sense of familiarity would enhance or detract from accuracy in memory. It is possible that in some instances, familiarity will enhance an eyewitness' memory, and in other situations familiarity will lead the eyewitness astray.

Consider the case of Chamar Avery. He was charged and convicted of murder based, in part, on faulty eyewitness identification (The National Registry of Exonerations, 2019). The case was a robbery turned murder, with only one eyewitness. The eyewitness claimed she knew one of the perpetrators in that they grew up in the same neighborhood (The National Registry of Exonerations, 2019). Chamar Avery was charged and convicted of murder in 2000, and he was sentenced to 20–50 years in prison. He was not exonerated for another 10 years, thus spending 10 years in prison for a crime he did not commit.

In contrast, as discussed in Chapter 1, Elizabeth Smart was abducted in the middle of the night, and the sole eyewitness to the crime was her younger sister, Mary Katherine. Although Mary Katherine did not get a good view of the perpetrator's face, she vaguely remembered the voice of the kidnapper because it sounded familiar to her—she just could not quite place it. Time passed, and as she was reading a book on world records, a photograph triggered her memory of who the abductor was. She gave a name and was able to tell her parents that it was one of the men who did some work for them at the house (Smart & Smart, 2003). Mary Katherine was in fact accurate with her "familiar" memory.

Theme 4

We cannot underestimate the degree to which an eyewitness/victim who claims to be familiar with the perpetrator is influential with a judge and/or jury. We need to understand whether special instructions or other remedies are necessary to educate judges/jurors of the influential nature of familiarity. Moreover, we need to gain a better understanding of how a witness' confidence is influenced by perceived familiarity and the impact of this level of confidence and familiarity on juror decision-making. Is there any need for expert testimony around these issues? Juror and jury decision-making research is essential for a more fulsome understanding of familiarity and confidence.

The Importance of Studying Familiarity in Terms of the Criminal Justice System

Given the frequency with which eyewitnesses/victims claim familiarity with perpetrators (Flowe, Mehta, & Ebbesen, 2011; Gross, Jacoby, Matheson, Montgomery, & Patil, 2005), it is imperative that we conduct research around familiar-stranger paradigms. We should also pay particular attention to real-life variables that co-occur with familiarity so that we can start to understand interactions around a highly complex phenomenon. By examining combinations of factors, we can provide best practices for claims of familiarity. Once comprehensive research on these topics is obtained, we also may be able to provide policy recommendations such that this type of eyewitness evidence is given appropriate consideration for just outcomes.

Conclusion

This book represents a consolidation of the psychological research to date on the construct of familiarity between an eyewitness and a perpetrator. At times, the eyewitness is accurate in claiming his or her sense of familiarity, whereas there are other times when this sense of familiarity is incorrect. Our goal was to describe the research currently available on the topic as well as identify the numerous gaps in the literature. We hope that researchers will pursue scholarship in the various avenues proposed. We urge that the next 100 years of eyewitness research focus on the "familiar-stranger."

References

Fisher, R. P., & Geiselman, R. E. (1992). *Memory-enhancing techniques for investigative interviewing: The cognitive interview.* Springfield, IL: Charles C Thomas.

Flowe, H. R., Mehta, A., & Ebbesen, E. B. (2011). The role of eyewitness identification evidence in felony case dispositions. *Psychology, Public Policy, and Law, 17,* 140–159. doi:10.1097/a00121311

Gronlund, S. D., Carlson, C. A., Dailey, S. B., & Goodsell, C. A. (2009). Robustness of the sequential lineup advantage. *Journal of Experimental Psychology: Applied, 15,* 140–152. doi:10.1037/a0015082

Gross, S. R., Jacoby, K., Matheson, D. J., Montgomery, N., & Patil, S. (2005). Exonerations in the United States 1989 through 2003. *Journal of Criminal Law and Criminology, 95*(2), 523–560.

Lindsay, R. C. L., & Wells, G. L. (1985). Improving eyewitness identification from lineups: Simultaneous and sequential lineup presentation. *Journal of Applied Psychology, 70,* 556–564.

Miethe, T., & Drass, K. (1999). Exploring the social context of instrumental and expressive homicides: An application of qualitative comparative analysis. *Journal of Quantitative Criminology, 1,* 1–21. doi:10.1023/A:1007550704282

Sheahan, C. L., & Pozzulo, J. D. (2019). *"I know that guy!": Familiarity, lineup procedure, and the adolescent witness.* Unpublished manuscript.

Smart, E., & Smart, L. (2003). *Bringing Elizabeth home: A journey of faith and hope.* New York, NY: Doubleday.

Steblay, N. L., Dysart, J. E., & Wells, G. L. (2015). An unrepresentative sample is unrepresentative regardless of the reason: A rejoinder to Amendola and Wixted. *Journal of Experimental Criminology, 11,* 295–298. doi:10.1007/s11292-015-9233-z

The National Registry of Exonerations. (2019). *Chamar Avery*. Retrieved January 29, 2019, from http://www.law.umich.edu/special/exoneration/Pages/casedetail.aspx?caseid=3825

Wells, G. L. (1978). Applied eyewitness-testimony research. System variables and estimator variables. *Journal of Personality and Social Psychology, 36*, 1546–1557. doi:http://dx.doi.org/10.1037/0022-3514.36.12.1546

Wells, G. L., Dysart, J. E., & Steblay, N. K. (2015). The flaw in Amendola and Wixted's conclusion on simultaneous versus sequential lineups. *Journal of Experimental Criminology, 11*, 285–289. doi:10.1007/s11292-014-9225-4

Index

References to figures are denoted by an italic *f* following the page number.
For the benefit of digital users, indexed terms that span two pages (e.g., 52–53) may, on occasion, appear on only one of those pages.